# Is Jesus the Savior?

~

A Journal Bible Study of Prophecies
Fulfilled in the Gospel of Matthew

~

For Beginners and Seekers

Includes the Complete Gospel of Matthew

SANDY K. COOK

**Published by Psalm 30 Publishing,**
© 2019 Sandra K. Cook, All rights reserved.

**Cover Photo credit:** https://www.pexels.com/@pixabay, "Barley Field Wheat Harvest," used under Free to use, public domain open license, with no attribution required; https://pixabay.com/users/kangbch-3007100.

**ISBN-13: 978-1-948953-03-0**

No part of this book may be copied or distributed by any means whatsoever. It is not to be copied electronically, by photocopy or reproduced in digital format. The contents of this book are protected by U.S. Copyright laws, and may not be reproduced without explicit written permission from Psalm 30 Publishing. Requests for permissions may be addressed to:

Psalm 30 Publishing,
P.O. Box 491328,
Lawrenceville, GA 30049

Unless otherwise noted, Bible verses printed in this book are taken from translations of the Bible that are in the Public Domain. Verses have been taken from an ASV-based, Public Domain translation, and have been modified to eliminate the use of the formal name of God. Within this book, God is addressed as God, The Lord, or Jesus throughout the book. As required by the Public Domain permissions of the secondary Public Domain source, the specific secondary Public Domain source will remain unidentified in this publication, because some of the verses have been modified and no longer directly reflect the content of the specific public domain source.

# DEDICATION

This book is dedicated to all who are seeking the truth, seeking God, or seeking to know Jesus. Being introduced to Jesus can fundamentally change your life and how you view the world as you learn more about Jesus. He will continue to change your character to better reflect the Holiness of God. I pray that you, my Dear Reader, will experience heartfelt transformations in your life and character as you pursue and get to know Jesus. May His light shine within you and into your life, so you are filled with the joy God meant for us to have from the beginning. You, Dear One, are beloved of God, and so I dedicate this book to YOU.

# ACKNOWLEDGMENTS

First and foremost, I'd like to acknowledge Jesus Christ, who gives us life to the fullest and who gave me the gifts with which I'm able to develop Bible Studies to share with others. It is His Holy Spirit which enables me to faithfully write for Him, even when my life circumstances are challenging. ♥

My husband and sons earn acknowledgement and recognition too. They are lights in my life, bringing joy even when days are difficult, encouraging me and lifting me up. My guys enable me to stay focused on serving where God leads me. ♥

I'd also like to acknowledge the women in The Sisterhood at The Bridge Church Atlanta. They encouraged me greatly with their kind and loving words about my first Journal Bible Study, *Be a Person After God's Own Heart: A Chronological Journal Bible Study of David and the Psalms*. Their praise far exceeded any expectation I had of one of my Bible studies being well-received. Their encouragement inspires me to keep using the gifts and talents God gave me with boldness. ♥

Lastly, I'd like to acknowledge all of the young seekers who are struggling to find meaning in today's world. You remind me so much of myself, when I was young, and you are the reason I write for God. Jesus holds the answers to happiness and wholeness in your life.

Jesus' answers are revealed when we seek Him. Jesus also makes us better people when we let His Words, His Ways, and His Wisdom infiltrate our souls. May you find His Spirit present with you throughout this study.

Warmest Wishes for a great adventure with God, our Father, Jesus Christ, His Son, and the Holy Spirit, who will teach you the things you need to know as you read this story of Jesus. ♥

# Table of Contents

*A LOOK BEFORE YOU LEAP* ............................................................................1
*MATTHEW 1* ...............................................................................................7
*MATTHEW 2* .............................................................................................13
*MATTHEW 3* .............................................................................................19
*MATTHEW 4* .............................................................................................25
*MATTHEW 5* .............................................................................................31
*MATTHEW 6* .............................................................................................37
*MATTHEW 7* .............................................................................................43
*MATTHEW 8* .............................................................................................49
*MATTHEW 9* .............................................................................................55
*MATTHEW 10*............................................................................................61
*MATTHEW 11*............................................................................................67
*MATTHEW 12*............................................................................................73
*MATTHEW 13*............................................................................................81
*MATTHEW 14*............................................................................................89
*MATTHEW 15*............................................................................................95
*MATTHEW 16*..........................................................................................101
*MATTHEW 17*..........................................................................................107
*MATTHEW 18*..........................................................................................113
*MATTHEW 19*..........................................................................................119
*MATTHEW 20*..........................................................................................125
*MATTHEW 21*..........................................................................................133
*MATTHEW 22*..........................................................................................141
*MATTHEW 23*..........................................................................................147
*MATTHEW 24*..........................................................................................153
*MATTHEW 25*..........................................................................................159
*MATTHEW 26*..........................................................................................165
*MATTHEW 27*..........................................................................................175
*MATTHEW 28*..........................................................................................183
*BONUS: ISAIAH 52:13-53* .......................................................................189
*BONUS: PSALM 22* .................................................................................193
*WHAT'S NEXT?* ......................................................................................199
*ABOUT THE AUTHOR*..............................................................................203

# A LOOK BEFORE YOU LEAP

## How Can We Know If Jesus Really Is THE Savior?

Can you know if Jesus is the Savior? Your Savior?

Hundreds of years before Jesus came to Earth, God's prophets wrote about a Savior God revealed to them. God gave us His Word in the Bible, so we can KNOW who is the Savior of the world.

Many prophesies were recorded in ancient Jewish scriptures. Those scriptures are in the Old Testament portion of the Christian Bible. In them, God told us what the Savior would be like and what His life would be like. God described The Savior and the circumstances of His life in detail.

As you get to know Jesus through this Bible study, you will learn what Jesus did, said, and taught while He was living on earth. You will gain confidence in knowing whether you believe Jesus is really the one and only Messiah as the scriptures described the Messiah—or not.

You may also wonder, how the prophesies in the book of Matthew relate to Jesus? The prophecies will be presented at the end of each chapter. My hope is that you will gain more understanding, and it will help you decide whether you believe the prophecies actually describe Jesus.

When Jesus was born, many ordinary Jewish people noticed Jesus' circumstances matched the Messiah described in the ancient prophesies. However, many chief priests and elders in the Jewish temples refused to recognize Jesus as the Messiah. So one big question is: Why did temple leaders reject Jesus as the Messiah? In this study of the book of Matthew, you'll learn why the chief priests and scribes hated Jesus so much, and ended up killing Him.

It's important to note: Jesus cannot be "just a great prophet," as some say. Jesus either told the truth or He lied. If Jesus lied, He can't be a great prophet because great prophets don't lie.

If Jesus told the truth about Himself, God's Word, and the prophecies, and He fulfilled those prophecies, then Jesus asks us to make a decision: Do you believe He is the resurrected son of God? It's totally your decision, but it's also an important decision to make.

# What Kind of Bible Study is This?

This is an open-ended, reflective, and life-application Journal Bible Study. It's a combination book, journal, and workbook.

The study is open-ended and reflective, because it is designed to let God's Holy Spirit teach you what He wants YOU to know. Many of the questions will help you explore how God's Word applies to your individual life.

In this study, you won't find lengthy explanations about the theological meaning of each passage. Nor will you find my interpretations or strong direction about how you should think of the Bible verses. Instead, you are encouraged to pray and ask God for insight into His word as it applies to you and your life.

If you are in a Bible study group, discussing each person's insights can be eye-opening. That's because everyone gains different insights from a study like this.

If you don't belong to a Bible study group, feel free to use resources, like Bible commentaries, to gain insight. You can also gain understanding by rereading the texts as needed. God made the Bible to be understood by common people, so everyone will gain a measure of personal insights from this study.

What you get out of each chapter will be between you and God. Your takeaways will depend upon your life circumstances, as well as how purposefully you seek to understand God's Word.

Lastly, this is a God-directed Bible study. In other words, as you read, pray and ask God for insight. Ask Him to show you the things He wants you to see. God will bring to your mind ideas and truths that are personally meaningful to you.

One of the main features of this Bible study is that all of the chapters of the Gospel of Matthew are included. All you need is this book, a pen or pencil, and time to read and relate to God's Word.

Including the entire Book of Matthew serves two purposes. It makes studying more convenient, because you won't have to go back-and-forth between a workbook, journal, and your Bible. You can read the text and answer the questions right where you are in this workbook journal.

The second purpose for including the full text is for simplicity in studying. It can be difficult and time-consuming to locate passages in a Bible, especially if you're new to Bible study or unfamiliar with the Bible. Having to look up scriptures can affect your ability to grasp the deeper meaning in the verses.

By including the Bible text in this Journal, you can read continuously without stopping. Therefore, this Journal Bible Study is designed to be pain free—easy to use and easy to understand.

On a side note: even though this study includes the full Gospel of Matthew, it's good for you to have an actual Bible to read too. The Psalm 30 Journal Bible Study series is designed to make studying individual books of the Bible easier by covering one book at a time. However, the studies shouldn't be considered complete works in isolation from the rest of the Bible. All of the Bible, taken as a whole, is critical for understanding God.

If you don't have your own Bible, and aren't sure how to choose a translation that is easy for you to read, visit: http://christianonlinebiblestudy.com/how-to-choose-a-bible/.

The information on that webpage shows you how to select a version that is easy for you to use. There are samples of different translations, so you can pick the one you like best. Hopefully, you can find a translation that is easy for you to read.

# How To Use This Journal Bible Study

In this Journal Bible Study, each chapter covers one chapter in the Gospel of the Book of Matthew. There are no verse numbers, since Matthew originally wrote his story as a book without numbered verses. Removing verse numbers will let your reading flow smoothly. You can read Matthew's story like it was originally written.

Next to each column of story text, there is a wide margin for your note taking or journaling. The margin is designed for you to write down anything that comes to your mind as you read. You can use the journal area to make notes about:

- ➢ Questions you have,
- ➢ Your emotions and reactions,
- ➢ Your thoughts about Jesus' teachings and actions,
- ➢ Your reaction to Jesus' commands,
- ➢ How you feel the text relates to your life or your personal character,
- ➢ Or any thought which comes to mind while you're reading.

If you like to draw or color, the open space allows freedom to interact with the Bible text in any way you find helpful. You can highlight, underline, draw arrows, and mark things up!

The best way to use this study is to settle in where you'll be comfortable and read a chapter. Before you begin reading, take a few minutes to pray. Praying is simply talking to God, as if He were a friend sitting next to you. Since God is Spirit, He is with us at all times wherever we go. He will hear whatever you say or ask. You may want to pray something similar to this:

"Dear Lord, please open my mind and heart to understand whatever you want me to learn through this study today. Give me the knowledge and understanding I need. Please speak to my heart where I need to be touched. Help me see Jesus for who He truly is, and reveal Yourself to me. I ask you for wisdom, Lord! Amen."

After your prayer, you might find it helpful to start by reading the "What's Next?" section at the end of the previous chapter, especially if it's been a few days since you last read. Taking a moment to review will help you reconnect with the main focus for the chapter you are about to read.

Interact with what you read by writing down your thoughts and reactions. Freely write whatever comes to your mind, highlight, et cetera. Reading actively will help you remember the details.

At the end of each chapter, you will find a "**PROPHECIES IN THIS CHAPTER**" section, which lists the prophesies about Jesus and made by Jesus in the chapter. Consider each prophecy for a moment, then write down your personal thoughts in the "**WHAT STANDS OUT IN THESE PROPHECIES TO YOU?**" section.

The main reason we are looking at the prophecies is to decide whether we believe Jesus and His life circumstances fit the ancient descriptions of the Messiah. After examining the prophesies given hundreds of years before Jesus lived, people see the evidence, get to know Jesus, and they often become convinced Jesus is the Messiah. Hopefully this process will give you clarity about your beliefs.

It's also important for you to know Deuteronomy 18:18-22, within the Bible, tells us prophecies which are from God will come true. If someone tells a prophecy, and it doesn't come true, they did not speak from God, but from within themselves.

Deuteronomy 18:18-22 says, "You may say in your heart, 'How shall we know the word which The

Lord has not spoken?' When a prophet speaks in The Lord's name, if the thing doesn't follow, nor happen, that is the thing which The Lord has not spoken. The prophet has spoken it presumptuously." So, if the prophecies about Jesus come true, we KNOW they are from God. And if they're from God, we'd be wise to listen when God speaks.

After each Prophecy section, there are six reflective questions in the **"WHAT DO YOU THINK?"** section. This is an opportunity for you to explore how the chapter's content applies to your life, your actions, thoughts, and feelings. *Make this study personal. Make it about you and your relationship with God by taking time to think about what you're reading.*

Take the scriptures into your heart. Consider what the Bible verses mean to you personally. Ask God what He wants YOU to know. Then thoughtfully answer each of the questions.

If you have no immediate reaction or thought, pray over the question. Ask God for His insight. Ask Him to bring to your mind ideas about how the chapter and prophecies apply to you.

Quiet your spirit for a moment, and wait for meaningful insight to come into your mind. Take note of any thoughts the Holy Spirit brings to you. Pause and reflect on the questions, so meaningful things come to your mind.

Lastly, each chapter has a **"WHAT'S NEXT?"** section. This is a short preview of the upcoming chapter. In the What's Next section, there are brief insights into the next chapter's main event(s), main point(s), or points worth noting. These insights can help you transition from one chapter to the next, especially if it's been a few days since you read the previous chapter.

On that note, **"WHAT'S NEXT?"** for your first chapter of this Journal Bible Study?

The Gospel of Matthew begins, by listing all of Jesus' ancestors and tells us about Jesus' birth. While the genealogy of Jesus is likely to be the least engaging reading in this entire study, notice the ancestors listed in the very first paragraph. Some of them come up in later prophecies, and some of the people in Jesus' ancestry tree are people just like you and me.

Jesus' birth story seems incredible. However, if you believe there is a God, it makes sense to believe God can do or create anything. Since God gives life, it's no surprise that He can spark life in the womb of a woman without a human man's involvement.

It's important to note also: all of the disciples who followed Jesus were Jewish men who knew the Messiah was coming. They believed Jesus was that person for which they had been waiting. As they followed Jesus, they became even more certain Jesus was the Messiah. Many of Jesus' disciples maintained their beliefs to the point of being killed by religious leaders, as was Jesus.

As a brief aside before diving into the study, let's see who was Matthew, besides the author of the Book of Matthew.

# Who was Matthew?

Matthew was a Jewish man who worked as a tax collector. He was called Levi in the Bible before he began to follow Jesus. We don't know why Matthew's name was changed when he began following Jesus, but the meaning of the name Matthew was given is "gift" or "gift of God."

As an individual, Matthew was one of the original 12 disciples who followed Jesus. Here is what the Bible says about Matthew's call to follow Jesus:

Matthew 9:9 says, "As Jesus passed by from there, he saw a man called Matthew sitting at the tax collection office. He said to him, 'Follow me.' He got up and followed him."

Luke 5:27-29 and Mark 2:14-16 describe the event similarly, but they both use Matthew's former name, Levi, in their accounts.

# The Gospel of Matthew's Authority

Matthew is one of many eye-witnesses who knew Jesus personally. He wrote about his personal experiences and shared his knowledge about the life of Jesus after Jesus was resurrected.

Having been raised in the Jewish faith, Matthew knew the ancient Jewish scriptures well. As a result, when Matthew wrote his account of Jesus' life, he incorporated ancient Jewish prophecies as proof of Jesus' Messiahship.

Matthew's Gospel carries strong authority, because it was written with the ancient Jewish scriptures as the foundation and it was written by one of Jesus' twelve chosen men. Matthew cites more prophecies than any of the other Gospel books.

Throughout Matthew's book, he indicates when specific events are the fulfillment of the prophecies. He often includes the Old Testament scriptures themselves as supporting documentation. Matthew's main goal was to document the ancient prophecies which point to Jesus as the true Messiah.

The four Gospel books (Matthew, Mark, Luke, and John) in the New Testament are well-written, early, authentic documents referenced by other first century writers. All four of the New Testament Gospels were written when people who actually knew Jesus were still alive.

The Gospels were written within the first century after Jesus lived. We have more timely supporting evidence for the Gospels than we do for writings of Caesar, Plato, Aristotle, and other ancient writings. Therefore, the Gospels are considered highly reliable documents about Jesus. (Visit https://carm.org/manuscript-evidence for information about dating of the Gospel manuscripts as supporting evidence.)

The impact of the prophecies on you will depend upon whether you believe them, whether you pray for insight and understanding from God as you read, and the personal insights God gives you. It also depends on how deep is your desire for a connection with God and your openness toward learning whatever God wants you to learn.

In Matthew 7:7 Jesus tells us, "Ask, and it will be given you. Seek, and you will find. Knock, and it will be opened for you." So ASK God to help you see the truth in His Word.

Remember, praying to God is just like talking to a good friend sitting next to you, whether you speak it aloud, or whether you just express yourself to God with words in your mind. This means, at any point in your reading, you can stop and pray. Doing so frequently will help you gain deeper understanding.

My hope in developing this Journal Bible Study is that you will receive the news of Jesus' messiahship in Matthew's Gospel with clarity. I hope you are inspired by the Gospel message, and you find this is a worthwhile journey through the Book of Matthew.

Are you ready to learn *Is Jesus The Savior*?

Let's dive into the book and prophecies to discover what God wants you to know..

# MATTHEW 1

The book of the genealogy of Jesus Christ, the son of David, the son of Abraham. Abraham became the father of Isaac. Isaac became the father of Jacob. Jacob became the father of Judah and his brothers. Judah became the father of Perez and Zerah by Tamar. Perez became the father of Hezron. Hezron became the father of Ram. Ram became the father of Amminadab. Amminadab became the father of Nahshon. Nahshon became the father of Salmon. Salmon became the father of Boaz by Rahab. Boaz became the father of Obed by Ruth. Obed became the father of Jesse. Jesse became the father of King David.

David became the father of Solomon by her who had been Uriah's wife. Solomon became the father of Rehoboam. Rehoboam became the father of Abijah. Abijah became the father of Asa. Asa became the father of Jehoshaphat. Jehoshaphat became the father of Joram. Joram became the father of Uzziah. Uzziah became the father of Jotham. Jotham became the father of Ahaz. Ahaz became the father of Hezekiah. Hezekiah became the father of Manasseh. Manasseh became the father of Amon. Amon became the father of Josiah.

Josiah became the father of Jechoniah and his brothers, at the time of the exile to Babylon. After the exile to Babylon, Jechoniah became the father of Shealtiel. Shealtiel became the father of Zerubbabel. Zerubbabel became the father of Abiud. Abiud became the father of Eliakim. Eliakim became the father of Azor. Azor became the father of Zadok. Zadok became the father of Achim. Achim became the father of Eliud. Eliud became the father of Eleazar. Eleazar became the father of Matthan. Matthan became the father of Jacob. Jacob became the father of Joseph, the husband of Mary, from whom was born Jesus, who is called Christ.

So all the generations from Abraham to David are fourteen generations; from David to the exile to Babylon fourteen generations; and from the carrying away to Babylon to the Christ, fourteen generations.

Now the birth of Jesus Christ was like this: After his mother, Mary, was engaged to Joseph, before they came together, she was found pregnant by the Holy Spirit.

Joseph, her husband, being a righteous man, and not willing to make her a public example, intended to put her away secretly. But when he thought about these things, behold, an angel of the Lord appeared to him in a dream, saying, "Joseph, son of David, don't be afraid to take to yourself Mary, your wife, for that which is conceived in her is of the Holy Spirit. She shall give birth to a son. You shall name him Jesus, for it is he who shall save his people from their sins."

Now all this has happened that it might be fulfilled which was spoken by the Lord through the prophet, saying,

"Behold, the virgin shall be with child, and shall give birth to a son. They shall call his name Immanuel;" which is, being interpreted, "God with us."

Joseph arose from his sleep, and did as the angel of the Lord commanded him, and took his wife to himself; and didn't know her sexually until she had given birth to her firstborn son. He named him Jesus.

# PROPHECIES IN THIS CHAPTER

**2 Samuel 7:12-16** – "When your days are fulfilled, and you sleep with your fathers, I will set up your offspring after you, who will proceed out of your body, and I will establish his kingdom. He will build a house for my name, and **I will establish the throne of his kingdom forever. I will be his father, and he will be my son**. If he commits iniquity, I will chasten him with the rod of men, and with the stripes of the children of men; but my loving kindness will not depart from him, as I took it from Saul, whom I put away before you. Your house and your kingdom will be made sure forever before you. Your throne will be established forever."

**Isaiah 7:14** – "Therefore the Lord himself will give you a sign. Behold, **the virgin will conceive**, and bear a son, and shall call his name Immanuel."

**Jeremiah 32:27** – "Behold, I am the Lord, the God of all flesh: is there anything too hard for me?"

**Psalm 132:11** – "The Lord has sworn to David in truth. He will not turn from it: 'I will set the fruit of your body on your throne.'"

**Isaiah 11:1** – "A shoot will come out of the stock of Jesse, and a branch out of his roots will bear fruit."

**Jeremiah 23:5** – "Behold, the days come, says The Lord, that I will raise to David a righteous Branch, and he shall reign as king and deal wisely, and shall execute justice and righteousness in the land."

**Genesis 22:18** – "All the nations of the earth will be blessed by your offspring, because you have obeyed my voice."

# WHY THESE PROPHECIES ARE IMPORTANT

Matthew begins his book with the genealogy of Jesus, because ancient prophecy said God would establish the Throne of David forever through David's Offspring. This is an important fact about the true Messiah, which God established long before Jesus was born. The prophecies about the Messiah's identification helps us recognize possible candidates for Messiah, because any candidate must be a descendant of David.

Since both Mary and Joseph are descendants 42 generations after King David lived, we know Jesus meets this genealogical criteria to be the real Messiah. The additional prophecies in Psalm 132, Isaiah 11, and in Jeremiah 23 affirm God's promise that the Messiah will come through the line of David, and he will be a righteous King.

In regard to David's throne being established forever, people still worship Jesus as their Lord and Savior more than 2000 years after Jesus was born. It's pretty safe to say that Jesus's kingdom, and thereby David's Kingdom, have been established forever.

The prophecy in Isaiah, says the Messiah will be born of a virgin. This is also a distinct characteristic of the Messiah. By all biblical accounts, Jesus was born of the Virgin Mary. Muslims, Protestants, Catholics, Mormons, and the Baha'i faith all believe Jesus was born of a virgin.

The key to deciding upon the validity of Isaiah's prophecy is to determine whether you believe God can independently spark life in an egg in the womb of a woman. Do you believe anything is too hard for God to do? If you believe God can initiate life independently in a woman's womb, it's worth noting that this claim has been made for Jesus's birth alone among men who claimed to be the Messiah.

Even further back in the Old Testament, God promises Abraham that all of the nations on earth will be blessed by His offspring. The line of David comes through Abraham and his son Isaac. So the long-awaited Messiah would be a descendant of both Abraham and of King David, of which is Jesus.

# WHAT STANDS OUT IN THESE PROPHECIES TO YOU?

_____
_____
_____
_____
_____
_____
_____

# WHAT DO YOU THINK?

➢ Go through Jesus's lineage at the beginning of Chapter 1 and circle the names of ancestors which you recognize. If you have time, briefly search on BibleHub.com or BibleGateway.com to learn more about the ancestors of Jesus. What surprises you about Jesus's ancestors?

_____
_____
_____
_____
_____
_____
_____

➢ Jesus's genealogy includes a prostitute, a widowed Moabite woman, Bathsheba with whom King David committed adultery, and virgin Mary. Some of Jesus' ancestors walked in the ways of the Lord; others turned their backs on God. How does Jesus's family background show His family is like our own families? How does this show our family backgrounds don't have to be perfect?

_____
_____
_____
_____
_____
_____
_____

- It was more than A Thousand Years after God's promise to David before David's Throne was established through Jesus. When God takes a long time to fulfill his promises, it can cause us to have doubts. How does the delay between a promise and its fulfillment affect the strength of your faith?

- Isaiah 7:14 says, "Therefore the Lord himself will give you a sign. Behold the Virgin shall conceive and bear a son and shall call his name Immanuel." God gave this explicit sign, plainly stated 800 years before Jesus was born. If people believe in God, and believe God created everything in the world, why do you suppose it's difficult for people to believe God caused Jesus to be born from a virgin?

- On a scale of absolute truth to total unbelief, how would you describe your level of faith that Jesus was born from a virgin? What affects your belief?

- The first two explicit signs about the Messiah are fulfilled in Matthew 1. Jesus is from the line of David and He is born of a virgin. God gave us these prophetic signs hundreds of years ago. Since God is unchanging, and He still expects us to accept the prophecies as proof of the Messiah today, what do you think God expects us to do with this evidence when it is revealed to us?

_____
_____
_____
_____
_____
_____
_____

# ACTION ITEM:

Pray about the doubts you have in believing some of the ancient prophecies, if any. Ask God to open your eyes to see and your ears to hear the truths He presented in the ancient prophecies. Ask God to strengthen your ability to see His truths.

# WHAT'S NEXT?

In the next chapter, Matthew 2, the scriptures lightly cover the childhood of Jesus. Matthew's synopsis of Jesus' early childhood is limited to the events which occurred as the fulfillment of ancient prophecies.

The early slaughter of infants in Bethlehem by King Herod, and Jesus' movements to and from Egypt are covered. With each of these events, Matthew references ancient prophecies. These references help us see how these events fulfilled prophesies in the life of Jesus.

Each additional prophecy, which is fulfilled in Jesus' life, further affirms whether He is the Messiah, the promised Savior of the world.

# MATTHEW 2

Now when Jesus was born in Bethlehem of Judea in the days of King Herod, behold, wise men from the east came to Jerusalem, saying, "Where is he who is born King of the Jews? For we saw his star in the east, and have come to worship him." When King Herod heard it, he was troubled, and all Jerusalem with him. Gathering together all the chief priests and scribes of the people, he asked them where the Christ would be born. They said to him, "In Bethlehem of Judea, for this is written through the prophet,

'You Bethlehem, land of Judah, are in no way least among the princes of Judah: for out of you shall come a governor, who shall shepherd my people, Israel.' "

Then Herod secretly called the wise men, and learned from them exactly what time the star appeared.

He sent them to Bethlehem, and said, "Go and search diligently for the young child. When you have found him, bring me word, so that I also may come and worship him."

They, having heard the king, went their way; and behold, the star, which they saw in the east, went before them, until it came and stood over where the young child was. When they saw the star, they rejoiced with exceedingly great joy. They came into the house and saw the young child with Mary, his mother, and they fell down and worshiped him. Opening their treasures, they offered to him gifts: gold, frankincense, and myrrh. Being warned in a dream not to return to Herod, they went back to their own country another way.

Now when they had departed, behold, an angel of the Lord appeared to Joseph in a dream, saying, "Arise and take the young child and his mother, and flee into Egypt, and stay there until I tell you, for Herod will seek the young child to destroy him."

He arose and took the young child and his mother by night, and departed into Egypt, and was there until the death of Herod; that it might be fulfilled which was spoken by the Lord through the prophet, saying, "Out of Egypt I called my son."

Then Herod, when he saw that he was mocked by the wise men, was exceedingly angry, and sent out, and killed all the male children who were in Bethlehem and in all the surrounding countryside, from two years old and under, according to the exact time which he had learned from the wise men. Then that which was spoken by Jeremiah the prophet was fulfilled, saying,

"A voice was heard in Ramah, lamentation, weeping and great mourning, Rachel weeping for her children; she wouldn't be comforted, because they are no more."

But when Herod was dead, behold, an angel of the Lord appeared in a dream to Joseph in Egypt, saying, "Arise and take the young child and his mother, and go into the land of Israel, for those who sought the young child's life are dead."

He arose and took the young child and his mother, and came into the land of Israel. But when he heard that Archelaus was reigning over Judea in the place of his father, Herod, Joseph was afraid to go there. Being warned in a dream, he withdrew into the region of Galilee, and came and lived in a city called Nazareth; that it might be fulfilled which was spoken through the prophets that he will be called a Nazarene.

## PROPHECIES IN THIS CHAPTER

**Numbers 24:17** – "I see him, but not now. I see him, but not near. A star will come out of Jacob. A scepter will rise out of Israel, and shall strike through the corners of Moab, and break down all the sons of Sheth."

**Isaiah 60:6** – "A multitude of camels will cover you, the dromedaries of Midian and Ephah. All from Sheba will come. They will bring gold and frankincense, and will proclaim the praises of The Lord."

**Micah 5:2** – "But you, Bethlehem Ephrathah, being small among the clans of Judah, out of you one will come out to me that is to be ruler in Israel; whose goings out are from of old, from ancient times."

**Genesis 49:10** – "The scepter will not depart from Judah, nor the ruler's staff from between his feet, until he comes to whom it belongs. To him will the obedience of the peoples be."

**Hosea 11:1** – "When Israel was a child, then I loved him, and called my son out of Egypt."

**Jeremiah 31:15** – "The Lord says: A voice is heard in Ramah, lamentation, and bitter weeping, Rachel weeping for her children; she refuses to be comforted for her children, because they are no more."

**Isaiah 53:3** – "He was despised, and rejected by men; a man of suffering, and acquainted with disease. He was despised as one from whom men hide their face; and we didn't respect him."

## WHY THESE PROPHECIES ARE IMPORTANT

Most of the prophecies in this chapter mention the geographical cities where the Messiah would come from and to which He would travel. In particular Bethlehem and Egypt are mentioned.

Micah 5:2 established that the Messiah would come from Bethlehem in the land of Judah. Numbers 24:17 and Genesis 49:10 also speak of the Messiah coming from Jacob's people in the land of Judah.

Hosea 11:1 established that the Messiah would spend time in the land of Egypt and be called out of Egypt. Since Jesus was taken there for a period of time, this prophecy is fulfilled in Jesus' upbringing.

When Herod kills all of the male children, aged two or younger, with the goal of killing Jesus, we see that Jesus is despised and rejected even as a toddler. Jeremiah 31:15 prophesied the devastating events which took place when Herod killed the male children. And Isaiah 53:3 tells us that the Messiah would be rejected and despised.

These descriptions and unique events in Jesus's childhood begin adding prophecies upon prophecies, which makes it statistically more likely Jesus is indeed the Messiah. For a person to fulfill one, two, or a few prophecies can be coincidental, but the Biblical prophesies go beyond statistical possibilities.

Professor Peter Stoner calculated the chances of one person fulfilling eight biblical prophecies would be one in one hundred quadrillion (1 in 1,000,000,000,000,000). Jesus fulfilled far more than eight ancient prophecies, so Prof. Stoner concluded it's a statistical impossibility for anyone else to come along who will fulfill as many prophecies as did Jesus.

As we continue our study, it becomes increasingly unlikely it is that anyone else will ever fulfill the prophecies like Jesus. His life, the historical events, and the circumstances were all very unique, and can never occur this way again in history, as you will learn through upcoming prophecies.

# WHAT STANDS OUT IN THESE PROPHECIES TO YOU?

_____
_____
_____
_____
_____
_____
_____

# WHAT DO YOU THINK?

➤ What are some ways the wise men could have known "the King of the Jews" was born?

_____
_____
_____
_____
_____
_____
_____

➤ Since Herod asked where the Christ child would be born, Herod knew of the Jewish prophecy. What do you think troubled Herod when he heard the King of the Jews had been born?

_____
_____
_____
_____
_____
_____

➤ Based on your thoughts and what you know about ordinary dreams, what characteristics of a dream would make it clear that a dream is from God, rather than being an ordinary dream?

_____
_____
_____
_____
_____
_____

➢ God brought the Israelites out of Egypt (Exodus 3-14) when they were slaves, and called them into freedom. God called Jesus into Egypt for a period of time, then called Him out of Egypt. What symbolic significance, if any, can you see in Jesus being called into and out of the land of slavery?

_____
_____
_____
_____
_____
_____
_____

➢ At the time Herod killed all of the male children in Jerusalem, do you think the common people recognized the slaughter as a fulfillment of the prophecy in Jeremiah 31:15? Why or why not?

_____
_____
_____
_____
_____
_____
_____

➢ Joseph immediately responded to the directions he received from God in his dreams telling him to move his family. If you had a dream where God told you to move, what factors would compel you to move as soon as God directed you to do so? What would make you hesitate to move?

_____
_____
_____
_____
_____
_____
_____

# ACTION ITEM:

Ask God if there is anything He wishes for you to do. Pause and sit in silence for a few moments after asking, and write down anything that comes to mind. Pray for further for clarity and confirmation, as needed.

_____
_____
_____
_____
_____
_____
_____
_____

# WHAT'S NEXT?

In Chapter 3 of Matthew, you will meet John the Baptist, who is Jesus' cousin. Ancient prophecies said one would come before the Messiah, who would be calling out in the wilderness to make way for the Lord.

As you read, think about whether you believe John the Baptist is the one calling out in the wilderness. Another question to consider is: If John is the one making way for the Lord, why did Jesus want to be baptized by John?

Chapter 3 brings us to the beginning of Jesus' public life as an eternal teacher. Therefore, going forward from here, the chapters will focus on Jesus' teachings, His actions, and His Spirit.

# MATTHEW 3

In those days, John the Baptizer came, preaching in the wilderness of Judea, saying, "Repent, for the Kingdom of Heaven is at hand!" For this is he who was spoken of by Isaiah the prophet, saying,

"The voice of one crying in the wilderness, make the way of the Lord ready! Make his paths straight!"

Now John himself wore clothing made of camel's hair, with a leather belt around his waist. His food was locusts and wild honey.

Then people from Jerusalem, all of Judea, and all the region around the Jordan went out to him. They were baptized by him in the Jordan, confessing their sins. But when he saw many of the Pharisees and Sadducees coming for his baptism, he said to them, "You offspring of vipers, who warned you to flee from the wrath to come? Therefore produce fruit worthy of repentance! Don't think to yourselves, 'We have Abraham for our father,' for I tell you that God is able to raise up children to Abraham from these stones.

"Even now the ax lies at the root of the trees. Therefore every tree that doesn't produce good fruit is cut down, and cast into the fire.

I indeed baptize you in water for repentance, but he who comes after me is mightier than I, whose sandals I am not worthy to carry. He will baptize you in the Holy Spirit. His winnowing fork is in his hand, and he will thoroughly cleanse his threshing floor. He will gather his wheat into the barn, but the chaff he will burn up with unquenchable fire."

Then Jesus came from Galilee to the Jordan to John, to be baptized by him. But John would have hindered him, saying, "I need to be baptized by you, and you come to me?"

But Jesus, answering, said to him, *"Allow it now, for this is the fitting way for us to fulfill all righteousness."*

Then John allowed him. Jesus, when he was baptized, went up directly from the water: and behold, the heavens were opened to him. He saw the Spirit of God descending as a dove, and coming on him. Behold, a voice out of the heavens said, *"This is my beloved Son, with whom I am well pleased."*

## PROPHECIES IN THIS CHAPTER

**Isaiah 40:3-5** – "The voice of one who calls out, 'Prepare the way of the Lord in the wilderness! Make a level highway in the desert for our God. Every valley shall be exalted, and every mountain and hill shall be made low. The uneven shall be made level, and the rough places a plain. The Lord's glory shall be revealed, and all flesh shall see it together; for the mouth of The Lord has spoken it.'"

**Malachi 3:1** – "'Behold, I send my messenger, and he will prepare the way before me; and the Lord, whom you seek, will suddenly come to his temple; and the messenger of the covenant, whom you desire, behold, he comes!' says the Lord of Armies."

**John 1:33** – "I didn't recognize him, but he who sent me to baptize in water, he said to me, 'On whomever you will see the Spirit descending, and remaining on him, the same is he who baptizes in the Holy Spirit.'"

## WHY THESE PROPHECIES ARE IMPORTANT

If it weren't for the prophecy of Isaiah 40:3 John the Baptist would seem to be some random guy telling people to repent. However, Isaiah 40:3 gives us biblical assurance that John the Baptist is a prophet, whom God foretold in prophecy hundreds of years earlier.

In Chapter 3 of Matthew, the opening verse tells us that John the Baptist was in the wilderness of Judea, preaching and telling people to repent, because the Kingdom of Heaven is at hand. Isaiah 40:3 says, "The voice of one who calls out, 'Prepare the way of the Lord in the wilderness! Make a level Highway in the desert for our God."

Malachi 3:1, also tells there is a messenger that goes before the Lord. Thus, it becomes clear John the Baptist fulfills the prophecy of one calling out as God's messenger at the time Jesus began his ministry.

Additionally, John the Baptist was told ahead of time that he would see the Spirit descending on the One who baptizes in the Holy Spirit. Since John saw the spirit descend and remain on Jesus, we know that Jesus is the one who baptizes us in the Holy Spirit, if we believe John was God's messenger.

# WHAT STANDS OUT IN THESE PROPHECIES TO YOU?

# WHAT DO YOU THINK?

➤ To repent means you are sincerely sorry about your wrongdoing, and you have a heart's desire to stop sinning. Why do you think John the Baptist was telling people to repent because Jesus Christ had come to Earth?

➤ What do you believe is the wrath to come, of which John the Baptist spoke?

➢ What do you think it looks like when we produce fruit worthy of repentance? What significance is it that John says every tree that does not produce good fruit is cut down, and cast into the fire?

___

➢ John Baptized with water, but Jesus baptizes us in the Holy Spirit. Picture these two types of baptism in your mind. Describe all you think and feel about being baptized in the Holy Spirit.

___

➢ John says Jesus will thoroughly clean the threshing floor by gathering wheat into the barn and burning the chaff in unquenchable fire. The chaff represents unrepentant Sinners, and wheat represents repentant people. What can you do to ensure you are gathered as wheat?

___

➢ If you were present at Jesus's baptism, what do you think your reaction would be to the voice from heaven? In what ways would it shape or change your beliefs about Jesus?

___

# ACTION ITEM:

Ask God to show you sins for which you need to repent. Take time to pray and ask God for His forgiveness for your wrongdoings. Pray also for His protection from future sins.

If it helps, feel free to jot down sins for which you wish to repent:

_____
_____
_____
_____
_____
_____
_____
_____

# WHAT'S NEXT?

Jesus is carried away to be tempted in the desert. We know from scriptures that we are ALL tested and tempted as a means of testing our faith and refining our character. While God Himself never tempts us, and it is always Satan or our fleshly desires that bring temptation, God allows the tempting for our own development.

Here are a couple of scriptures about temptation:

**James 1:12** - "Blessed is the man who endures temptation, for when he has been approved, he will receive the crown of life, which the Lord promised to those who love him."

**James 1:2-4** - "Count it all joy, my brothers, when you fall into various temptations, knowing that the testing of your faith produces endurance. Let endurance have its perfect work, that you may be perfect and complete, lacking in nothing."

In the next chapter, look for Jesus' method for standing against temptation. As you read, consider how Jesus' method might help you stand against the temptations in your life.

# MATTHEW 4

Then Jesus was led up by the Spirit into the wilderness to be tempted by the devil. When he had fasted forty days and forty nights, he was hungry afterward. The tempter came and said to him, "If you are the Son of God, command that these stones become bread."

But he answered, *"It is written, 'Man shall not live by bread alone, but by every word that proceeds out of God's mouth.'"*

Then the devil took him into the holy city. He set him on the pinnacle of the temple, and said to him, "If you are the Son of God, throw yourself down, for it is written, 'He will command his angels concerning you,' and, 'On their hands they will bear you up, so that you don't dash your foot against a stone.'"

Jesus said to him, *"Again, it is written, 'You shall not test the Lord, your God.'"*

Again, the devil took him to an exceedingly high mountain, and showed him all the kingdoms of the world, and their glory. He said to him, "I will give you all of these things, if you will fall down and worship me."

Then Jesus said to him, *"Get behind me, Satan! For it is written, 'You shall worship the Lord your God, and you shall serve him only.'"*

Then the devil left him, and behold, angels came and served him. Now when Jesus heard that John was delivered up, he withdrew into Galilee. Leaving Nazareth, he came and lived in Capernaum, which is by the sea, in the region of Zebulun and Naphtali, that it might be fulfilled which was spoken through Isaiah the prophet, saying, "The land of Zebulun and the land of Naphtali, toward the sea, beyond the Jordan, Galilee of the Gentiles, the people who sat in darkness saw a great light, to those who sat in the region and shadow of death, to them light has dawned."

From that time, Jesus began to preach, and to say, *"Repent! For the Kingdom of Heaven is at hand."*

Walking by the sea of Galilee, he saw two brothers: Simon, who is called Peter, and Andrew, his brother, casting a net into the sea; for they were fishermen. He said to them, *"Come after me, and I will make you fishers for men."*

They immediately left their nets and followed him.

Going on from there, he saw two other brothers, James the son of Zebedee, and John his brother, in the boat with Zebedee their father, mending their nets. He called them. They immediately left the boat and their father, and followed him. Jesus went about in all Galilee, teaching in their synagogues, preaching the Good News of the Kingdom, and healing every disease and every sickness among the people. The report about him went out into all Syria. They brought to him all who were sick, afflicted with various diseases and torments, possessed with demons, epileptics, and paralytics; and he healed them. Great multitudes from Galilee, Decapolis, Jerusalem, Judea and from beyond the Jordan followed him.

# PROPHECIES IN THIS CHAPTER

**Isaiah 9:1-2** – "But there shall be no more gloom for her who was in anguish. In the former time, he brought into contempt the land of Zebulun and the land of Naphtali; but in the latter time he has made it glorious, by the way of the sea, beyond the Jordan, Galilee of the nations. The people who walked in darkness have seen a great light. Those who lived in the land of the shadow of death, on them the light has shined."

**Isaiah 42:1-7** – "Behold, my servant, whom I uphold; my chosen, in whom my soul delights—I have put my Spirit on him. He will bring justice to the nations.

He will not shout, nor raise his voice, nor cause it to be heard in the street.
He won't break a bruised reed.
He won't quench a dimly burning wick.
He will faithfully bring justice.
He will not fail nor be discouraged, until he has set justice in the earth, and the islands will wait for his law."

Thus says God The Lord,
 he who created the heavens and stretched them out,
 he who spread out the earth and that which comes out of it,
 he who gives breath to its people and spirit to those who walk in it.
"I, The Lord, have called you in righteousness, and will hold your hand, and will keep you, and make you a covenant for the people, as a light for the nations; to open the blind eyes, to bring the prisoners out of the dungeon, and those who sit in darkness out of the prison."

# WHY THESE PROPHECIES ARE IMPORTANT

After Satan tested Jesus with temptation in the desert, Jesus left Nazareth. He went into Galilee and lived in Capernaum in the region of Zebulun and Naphtali. Isaiah's 9:1-2 prophecy says a great light came into Galilee in the land of Zebulun and Naphtali.

The Messiah, Jesus, is frequently referred to as a light, the light of the world (John 8:12 & 9:5), and a light shining in the darkness (John 12:46 & Romans 12:19). The Bible says God is light (1 John 1:5).

This prophecy in Isaiah 9 is a bit obscure, since it refers to a light coming into the region. However historical Bible interpretation agrees the light which came into Galilee, in the region of Zebulun and Naphtali, is a reference to the Messiah. Thus, Jesus fulfills this prophecy when He settles in Galilee.

Isaiah 42:1-7 describes the Messiah in more detail. This passage speaks of the character of the Messiah. He is not yelling, bruising, nor quenching people's spirits. Jesus is a strong and faithful encourager.

As Jesus begins his ministry, we see Jesus is starting to heal people's diseases, restoring them, helping them, and we begin to see the individual character of Jesus. The passage from Isaiah 42 helps us see how Jesus's character matches that of the prophesied Messiah.

# WHAT STANDS OUT IN THESE PROPHECIES TO YOU?

_____
_____
_____
_____
_____
_____
_____

# WHAT DO YOU THINK?

➢ Jesus was tempted by human needs and desires. With what temptations do you struggle?

_____
_____
_____
_____
_____

➢ Based on how Jesus quoted God's Word, how can God's Word help us live more righteously?

_____
_____
_____
_____
_____
_____
_____

➢ Jesus was tempted by Satan, but He defended himself by quoting scripture. What are some ways you can be more prepared to withstand temptations? (See also Ephesians 6:10-18)

_____
_____
_____
_____
_____
_____

➢ If Jesus brings light into a dark world, why do many people reject His light coming into their lives?

_____
_____
_____
_____
_____
_____

➢ If Jesus walked by you and said, "Come after me," would you immediately leave everything and follow Him? Why did you answer the way that you did?

_____
_____
_____
_____
_____
_____
_____

➢ When Jesus performed miracles of healing, a multitude of people began to follow him. With all you know about Jesus so far, for what reasons you think multitudes started following Jesus?

_____
_____
_____
_____
_____
_____
_____

# ACTION ITEM:

See if you can find a Bible reading plan or a memorization app to help you soak God's Word into your soul. You can find either of these through searches online. Make a commitment to begin regularly using the tool you selected.

# WHAT'S NEXT?

In the next chapter, Jesus holds His first public speaking event in front of a huge crowd. This first speech is called the Sermon on the Mount. It begins with the Beatitudes, which are nine "Blessed are.." statements Jesus makes at the beginning of His speech.

Take note of the differences between what Jesus tells us to do versus common actions or reactions, which people typically have in today's world.

As you read, circle the passages in Jesus' speech which speak to your heart about something you deal with in your life.

# MATTHEW 5

Seeing the multitudes, he went up onto the mountain.

When he had sat down, his disciples came to him. He opened his mouth and taught them, saying,

*"Blessed are the poor in spirit, for theirs is the Kingdom of Heaven.*

*"Blessed are those who mourn, for they shall be comforted.*

*"Blessed are the gentle, for they shall inherit the earth.*

*"Blessed are those who hunger and thirst after righteousness, for they shall be filled.*

*"Blessed are the merciful, for they shall obtain mercy.*

*"Blessed are the pure in heart, for they shall see God.*

*"Blessed are the peacemakers, for they shall be called children of God.*

*"Blessed are those who have been persecuted for righteousness' sake, for theirs is the Kingdom of Heaven.*

*"Blessed are you when people reproach you, persecute you, and say all kinds of evil against you falsely, for my sake. Rejoice, and be exceedingly glad, for great is your reward in heaven. For that is how they persecuted the prophets who were before you.*

"You are the salt of the earth, but if the salt has lost its flavor, with what will it be salted? It is then good for nothing, but to be cast out and trodden under the feet of men. You are the light of the world. A city located on a hill can't be hidden.

"Neither do you light a lamp, and put it under a measuring basket, but on a stand; and it shines to all who are in the house. Even so, let your light shine before men; that they may see your good works, and glorify your Father who is in heaven.

"Don't think that I came to destroy the law or the prophets. I didn't come to destroy, but to fulfill. For most certainly, I tell you, until heaven and earth pass away, not even one smallest letter or one tiny pen stroke shall in any way pass away from the law, until all things are accomplished. Whoever, therefore, shall break one of these least commandments, and teach others to do so, shall be called least in the Kingdom of Heaven; but whoever shall do and teach them shall be called great in the Kingdom of Heaven. For I tell you that unless your righteousness exceeds that of the scribes and Pharisees, there is no way you will enter into the Kingdom of Heaven.

"You have heard that it was said to the ancient ones, 'You shall not murder;' and 'Whoever murders will be in danger of the judgment.' But I tell you that everyone who is angry with his brother without a cause will be in danger of the judgment. Whoever says to his brother, 'Raca!' will be in danger of the council. Whoever says, 'You fool!' will be in danger of the fire of Gehenna.

"If therefore you are offering your gift at the altar, and there remember that your brother has anything against you, leave your gift there before the altar, and go your way. First be reconciled to your brother, and then come and offer your gift. Agree with your adversary quickly, while you are with him on the way; lest perhaps the prosecutor deliver you to the judge, and the judge deliver you to the officer, and you be cast into prison. Most certainly I tell you, you shall by no means get out of there, until you have paid the last penny.

"You have heard that it was said, 'You shall not commit adultery;' but I tell you that everyone who gazes at a woman to lust after her has committed adultery with her already in his heart.

"If your right eye causes you to stumble, pluck it out and throw it away from you. For it is more profitable for you that one of your members should perish, than for your whole body to be cast into Gehenna.

"If your right hand causes you to stumble, cut it off, and throw it away from you. For it is more profitable for you that one of your members should perish, than for your whole body to be cast into Gehenna.

"It was also said, 'Whoever shall put away his wife, let him give her a writing of divorce,' but I tell you that whoever puts away his wife, except for the cause of sexual immorality, makes her an adulteress; and whoever marries her when she is put away commits adultery.

"Again you have heard that it was said to the ancient ones, 'You shall not make false vows, but shall perform to the Lord your vows,' but I tell you, don't swear at all: neither by heaven, for it is the throne of God; nor by the earth, for it is the footstool of his feet; nor by Jerusalem, for it is the city of the great King. Neither shall you swear by your head, for you can't make one hair white or black. But let your 'Yes' be 'Yes' and your 'No' be 'No.' Whatever is more than these is of the evil one.

"You have heard that it was said, 'An eye for an eye, and a tooth for a tooth.' But I tell you, don't resist him who is evil; but whoever strikes you on your right cheek, turn to him the other also. If anyone sues you to take away your coat, let him have your cloak also. Whoever compels you to go one mile, go with him two. Give to him who asks you, and don't turn away him who desires to borrow from you.

"You have heard that it was said, 'You shall love your neighbor and hate your enemy.' But I tell you, love your enemies, bless those who curse you, do good to those who hate you, and pray for those who mistreat you and persecute you, that you may be children of your Father who is in heaven. For he makes his sun to rise on the evil and the good, and sends rain on the just and the unjust. For if you love those who love you, what reward do you have? Don't even the tax collectors do the same?

"If you only greet your friends, what more do you do than others? Don't even the tax collectors do the same? Therefore you shall be perfect, just as your Father in heaven is perfect."

# PROPHECIES IN THIS CHAPTER

**Isaiah 61:1-3** – The Lord God's Spirit is on me; because God has anointed me to preach good news to the humble. He has sent me to bind up the broken hearted, to proclaim liberty to the captives, and release to those who are bound; to proclaim the year of The Lord's favor, and the day of vengeance of our God; to comfort all who mourn; to provide for those who mourn in Zion, to give to them a garland for ashes, the oil of joy for mourning, the garment of praise for the spirit of heaviness; that they may be called trees of righteousness, the planting of The Lord, that he may be glorified.

# WHY THIS PROPHECY IS IMPORTANT

The prophecy in Isaiah 61:1-3 tells us that the spirit of the Lord is going to be on the Messiah. He will preach good news and proclaim the Lord's favor. He will bind up the broken-hearted, proclaim liberty, and be an uplifting spirit to people in the world.

Here, in Matthew 5, we see that Jesus starts teaching and proclaiming God's message. From this prophecy, we know Isaiah accurately describes the way Jesus teaches and His actions. Isaiah confirms the affect the Messiah will have and which Jesus has had upon people with which He interacts.

# WHAT STANDS OUT IN THIS PROPHECY TO YOU?

_____
_____
_____
_____
_____
_____
_____
_____

# WHAT DO YOU THINK?

➢ What kinds of things can you do to shine your encouragement and light before other people?

_____
_____
_____
_____
_____
_____
_____

➤ Instead of making fun or getting angry with people, what does Jesus say we should do?

➤ Who do you know that holds past wrongdoing(s) against you? What would be a good first step in making amends with that person (or people)?

➤ How is lusting after someone like committing adultery, and how does lust harm a marriage?

➤ What harm results when we swear we will do something, but we don't actually do what we said?

➢ Why do you suppose Jesus wants us to love and be generous to enemies and evil people, rather than hating them, resisting them, or seeking revenge?

_____
_____
_____
_____
_____
_____

# ACTION ITEM:

Look back at Jesus' teachings in this chapter to see which of His teachings apply directly to problems or issues you have in your life. In the space provided here, list the area(s) of difficulty in your life, which you would like to improve. You will refer back to these items after reading Chapter 7.

_____
_____
_____
_____
_____

# WHAT'S NEXT?

In the next chapter, Jesus continues His Sermon on the Mount. Take note of the differences between what Jesus tells us to do versus common actions or reactions people have in today's world.

Again, as you read, circle each part of Jesus' speech which talks about something you deal with personally in your life. You will list those items at the end of the next chapter, just as you did with this chapter. These lists will be used in an action item coming up at the end of Chapter 7.

# MATTHEW 6

"Be careful that you don't do your charitable giving before men, to be seen by them, or else you have no reward from your Father who is in heaven. Therefore when you do merciful deeds, don't sound a trumpet before yourself, as the hypocrites do in the synagogues and in the streets, that they may get glory from men. Most certainly I tell you, they have received their reward. But when you do merciful deeds, don't let your left hand know what your right hand does, so that your merciful deeds may be in secret, then your Father who sees in secret will reward you openly.

"When you pray, you shall not be as the hypocrites, for they love to stand and pray in the synagogues and in the corners of the streets, that they may be seen by men. Most certainly, I tell you, they have received their reward. But you, when you pray, enter into your inner room, and having shut your door, pray to your Father who is in secret, and your Father who sees in secret will reward you openly.

"In praying, don't use vain repetitions, as the Gentiles do; for they think that they will be heard for their much speaking. Therefore don't be like them, for your Father knows what things you need, before you ask him. Pray like this:

'Our Father in heaven, may your name be kept holy. Let your Kingdom come. Let your will be done on earth as it is in heaven. Give us today our daily bread. Forgive us our debts, as we also forgive our debtors. Bring us not into temptation, but deliver us from the evil one. For yours is the Kingdom, the power, and the glory forever. Amen.'

"For if you forgive men their trespasses, your Heavenly Father will also forgive you. But if you don't forgive men their trespasses, neither will your Father forgive your trespasses.

"Moreover when you fast, don't be like the hypocrites, with sad faces. For they disfigure their faces, that they may be seen by men to be fasting. Most certainly I tell you, they have received their reward. But you, when you fast, anoint your head, and wash your face; so that you are not seen by men to be fasting, but by your Father who is in secret, and your Father, who sees in secret, will reward you.

"Don't lay up treasures for yourselves on the earth, where moth and rust consume, and where thieves break through and steal; but lay up for yourselves treasures in heaven, where neither moth nor rust consume, and where thieves don't break through and steal; for where your treasure is, there your heart will be also.

"The lamp of the body is the eye. If therefore your eye is sound, your whole body will be full of light. But if your eye is evil, your whole body will be full of darkness. If therefore the light that is in you is darkness, how great is the darkness!

"No one can serve two masters, for either he will hate the one and love the other; or else he will be devoted to one and despise the other. You can't serve both God and Mammon. Therefore I tell you, don't be anxious for your life: what you will eat, or what you will drink; nor yet for your body, what you will wear. Isn't life more than food, and the body more than clothing? See the birds of the sky, that they don't sow, neither do they reap, nor gather into barns. Your heavenly Father feeds them. Aren't you of much more value than they?

"Which of you, by being anxious, can add one moment to his lifespan? Why are you anxious about clothing? Consider the lilies of the field, how they grow.

*"They don't toil, neither do they spin, yet I tell you that even Solomon in all his glory was not dressed like one of these. But if God so clothes the grass of the field, which today exists, and tomorrow is thrown into the oven, won't he much more clothe you, you of little faith? "Therefore don't be anxious, saying, 'What will we eat?', 'What will we drink?' or, 'With what will we be clothed?' For the Gentiles seek after all these things; for your heavenly Father knows that you need all these things. But seek first God's Kingdom, and his righteousness; and all these things will be given to you as well. Therefore don't be anxious for tomorrow, for tomorrow will be anxious for itself. Each day's own evil is sufficient."*

## PROPHECIES IN THIS CHAPTER

NONE.

## WHAT DO YOU THINK?

➢ Why do you think Jesus says to do your good deeds and to pray in secret? What is wrong with making efforts to be seen praying in public or proclaiming your good deeds?

➢ Jesus clearly says, if you don't forgive others, God won't forgive you. Who might you need to forgive? What holds you back from forgiving, and how can you get past feeling unforgiving?

➢ Why is it hypocritical to outwardly display that you're fasting?

_____
_____
_____
_____
_____
_____
_____

➢ What treasures can you think of, which you will take to heaven with you? How can you lay up more of these kinds of treasures?

_____
_____
_____
_____
_____
_____
_____

➢ Why do you think it's impossible to serve both God and mammon (coveted wealth)?

_____
_____
_____
_____
_____
_____
_____

➢ What kinds of actions can you take to pursue God's Kingdom here on earth?

_____
_____
_____
_____
_____
_____
_____

# ACTION ITEM:

Look back at Jesus' teachings in this chapter. Which of His teachings apply directly to problems or issues which exist in your life? List area(s) of difficulty would you like to work on improving in the space provided here. You will refer back to these items after reading Chapter 7.

_____
_____
_____
_____
_____
_____
_____
_____
_____

# WHAT'S NEXT?

In the next chapter, Jesus concludes His Sermon on the Mount. Once again, notice the differences between what Jesus tells us to do versus the typical actions and reactions people have in today's world.

Also, as you read, circle each part of Jesus' speech which speaks to something you deal with personally in your life. You will list those items at the end of the chapter, just as you did with the previous two chapters.

The three lists of problems or issues in your life will be used in an action item at the end of the next chapter.

# MATTHEW 7

"Don't judge, so that you won't be judged. For with whatever judgment you judge, you will be judged; and with whatever measure you measure, it will be measured to you. Why do you see the speck that is in your brother's eye, but don't consider the beam that is in your own eye? Or how will you tell your brother, 'Let me remove the speck from your eye;' and behold, the beam is in your own eye? You hypocrite! First remove the beam out of your own eye, and then you can see clearly to remove the speck out of your brother's eye.

"Don't give that which is holy to the dogs, neither throw your pearls before the pigs, lest perhaps they trample them under their feet, and turn and tear you to pieces.

"Ask, and it will be given you. Seek, and you will find. Knock, and it will be opened for you. For everyone who asks receives. He who seeks finds. To him who knocks it will be opened. Or who is there among you, who, if his son asks him for bread, will give him a stone?

"Or if he asks for a fish, who will give him a serpent? If you then, being evil, know how to give good gifts to your children, how much more will your Father who is in heaven give good things to those who ask him! Therefore whatever you desire for men *to do to you, you shall also do to them; for this is the law and the prophets.*

*"Enter in by the narrow gate; for wide is the gate and broad is the way that leads to destruction, and many are those who enter in by it. How narrow is the gate, and restricted is the way that leads to life! Few are those who find it.*

*"Beware of false prophets, who come to you in sheep's clothing, but inwardly are ravening wolves. By their fruits you will know them. Do you gather grapes from thorns, or figs from thistles? Even so, every good tree produces good fruit; but the corrupt tree produces evil fruit. A good tree can't produce evil fruit, neither can a corrupt tree produce good fruit.*

*"Every tree that doesn't grow good fruit is cut down, and thrown into the fire. Therefore by their fruits you will know them. Not everyone who says to me, 'Lord, Lord,' will enter into the Kingdom of Heaven; but he who does the will of my Father who is in heaven.*

*"Many will tell me in that day, 'Lord, Lord, didn't we prophesy in your name, in your name cast out demons, and in your name do many mighty works?'*

*"Then I will tell them, 'I never knew you. Depart from me, you who work iniquity.'*

*"Everyone therefore who hears these words of mine, and does them, I will liken him to a wise man, who built his house on a rock. The rain came down, the floods came, and the winds blew, and beat on that house; and it didn't fall, for it was founded on the rock.*

*"Everyone who hears these words of mine, and doesn't do them will be like a foolish man, who built his house on the sand. The rain came down, the floods came, and the winds blew, and beat on that house; and it fell—and great was its fall."*

When Jesus had finished saying these things, the multitudes were astonished at his teaching, for he taught them with authority, and not like the scribes.

# PROPHECIES IN THIS CHAPTER

NONE.

# WHAT DO YOU THINK?

➤ Describe the kinds of judgments you tend to make when you interact with people you don't like:

_____
_____
_____
_____
_____
_____
_____
_____

➤ Since we are judged in the same way we judge others, how would you expect other people might judge you and treat you?

_____
_____
_____
_____
_____
_____
_____

➤ At this time in your life, do you think you will go through the wide gate or the narrow gate? What makes you think that?

_____
_____
_____
_____
_____
_____
_____

➤ What does the fruit of your life look like right now? What kind(s) of good fruit could you produce?

_____
_____
_____
_____
_____
_____
_____

➢ What does God want you to do and not to do? Refer to Exodus 20, Matthew 22:36-40, and Romans 8:28-29 at https://www.biblegateway.com, if you need help.

_____
_____
_____
_____
_____
_____

➢ Look back at Jesus' teachings in this chapter. Which of His teachings in this portion of the Sermon on the Mount apply to you?

_____
_____
_____
_____
_____
_____

# ACTION ITEM:

Look back at the lists you made at the end of chapters 5, 6, & 7. Decide which behavior(s) you would like to work on improving. What are some specific things you can do better in your selected area(s)?

_____
_____
_____
_____
_____

Pray and ask God to lead you to books, audiobooks, podcasts, courses, or a mentor who can help you overcome your areas of difficulty. Begin praying daily for God to help you!

Your awareness of your faults, added to your willingness to work on changing, means you have an open heart and mind toward improving yourself. God wants to help us become as close to being holy as possible, so He WILL help, if you ask Him! This is how God changes lives.

Take advantage of whatever resources you can find. Prayerfully work with God to improve in the areas of difficulty you're having.

# WHAT'S NEXT?

In the next chapter, Jesus begins traveling, healing people, and teaching multitudes regularly. Take note of some of the surprising things Jesus says about faith and fear. Pay close attention to the role of faith, as it relates to receiving what we desire.

# MATTHEW 8

When he came down from the mountain, great multitudes followed him. Behold, a leper came to him and worshiped him, saying, "Lord, if you want to, you can make me clean."

Jesus stretched out his hand, and touched him, saying, *"I want to. Be made clean."* Immediately his leprosy was cleansed. Jesus said to him, *"See that you tell nobody, but go, show yourself to the priest, and offer the gift that Moses commanded, as a testimony to them."*

When he came into Capernaum, a centurion came to him, asking him, and saying, "Lord, my servant lies in the house paralyzed, grievously tormented."

Jesus said to him, *"I will come and heal him."*

The centurion answered, "Lord, I'm not worthy for you to come under my roof. Just say the word, and my servant will be healed. For I am also a man under authority, having under myself soldiers. I tell this one, 'Go,' and he goes; and tell another, 'Come,' and he comes; and tell my servant, 'Do this,' and he does it."

When Jesus heard it, he marveled, and said to those who followed, *"Most certainly I tell you,*

*I haven't found so great a faith, not even in Israel. I tell you that many will come from the east and the west, and will sit down with Abraham, Isaac, and Jacob in the Kingdom of Heaven, but the children of the Kingdom will be thrown out into the outer darkness. There will be weeping and gnashing of teeth."*

Jesus said to the centurion, *"Go your way. Let it be done for you as you have believed."* His servant was healed in that hour.

When Jesus came into Peter's house, he saw his wife's mother lying sick with a fever. He touched her hand, and the fever left her. She got up and served him.

When evening came, they brought to him many possessed with demons. He cast out the spirits with a word, and healed all who were sick; that it might be fulfilled which was spoken through Isaiah the prophet, saying, "He took our infirmities, and bore our diseases."

Now when Jesus saw great multitudes around him, he gave the order to depart to the other side.

A scribe came, and said to him, "Teacher, I will follow you wherever you go."

Jesus said to him, *"The foxes have holes, and the birds of the sky have nests, but the Son of Man has nowhere to lay his head."*

Another of his disciples said to him, "Lord, allow me first to go and bury my father."

But Jesus said to him, *"Follow me, and leave the dead to bury their own dead."*

When he got into a boat, his disciples followed him.

Behold, a violent storm came up on the sea, so much that the boat was covered with the waves, but he was asleep. They came to him, and woke him up, saying,

"Save us, Lord! We are dying!"

He said to them, *"Why are you fearful, O you of little faith?"* Then he got up, rebuked the wind and the sea, and there was a great calm.

The men marveled, saying, "What kind of

man is this, that even the wind and the sea obey him?"

When he came to the other side, into the country of the Gergesenes, two people possessed by demons met him there, coming out of the tombs, exceedingly fierce, so that nobody could pass that way.

Behold, they cried out, saying, "What do we have to do with you, Jesus, Son of God? Have you come here to torment us before the time?" Now there was a herd of many pigs feeding far away from them. The demons begged him, saying, "If you cast us out, permit us to go away into the herd of pigs."

He said to them, *"Go!"*

They came out, and went into the herd of pigs: and behold, the whole herd of pigs rushed down the cliff into the sea, and died in the water. Those who fed them fled, and went away into the city, and told everything, including what happened to those who were possessed with demons. Behold, all the city came out to meet Jesus. When they saw him, they begged that he would depart from their borders.

# PROPHECIES IN THIS CHAPTER

**Isaiah 53:4** – "Surely he has borne our sickness, and carried our suffering; yet we considered him plagued, struck by God, and afflicted."

**Psalm 65:6-7** – "Who by his power forms the mountains, having armed yourself with strength; who stills the roaring of the seas, the roaring of their waves, and the turmoil of the nations."

**Psalm 107:20** – "He sends his word, and heals them, and delivers them from their graves."

# WHY THESE PROPHECIES ARE IMPORTANT

The prophecy in Isaiah 53:4 says, "Surely he has borne our sickness and carried suffering." Here in chapter 8 of Matthew, we read that Jesus cast out evil spirits and healed those that were sick. This prophecy is important because it told us the Messiah would do these things here on Earth.

Matthew 8 talks about Jesus's ministry as one primarily focused on healing people with a variety of health problems. In Matthew, we see Jesus is doing the work on Earth which the prophecies in Isaiah 53 and Psalm 107 said the Messiah would do.

We know from the passage in Psalm 65, God has power over the roaring seas and waves. Here in Matthew 8, when Jesus stills the waves by telling them to be calm, He demonstrates His power over the waters of the earth. This is a characteristic of God.

It just so happens, here in chapter 8, we also reach a point where Jesus has fulfilled more than eight prophecies. At this point, there is a <u>one in one hundred quadrillion</u> chance that Jesus (or any man) would have fulfilled eight prophecies. As we go forward from here, the prophecies become increasingly clear, and begin demonstrating they apply to Jesus alone as a person who has lived on earth. The prophecies fulfilled by Jesus in the last week of His life are astounding, as you will see in the chapters ahead.

## WHAT STANDS OUT IN THESE PROPHECIES TO YOU?

## WHAT DO YOU THINK?

➢ Jesus says many will sit down with Abraham, Isaac, and Jacob in the Kingdom of Heaven. Of the great people in the Bible, who would you want to sit with and what would you ask that person?

➢ Describe the typical strength of faith you have in God and Jesus. What affects your level of faith?

➢ List all of the Miracles of healing Jesus performed in this chapter. What surprises you about His miracles?

_____
_____
_____
_____
_____
_____

➢ One disciple wanted to delay following Jesus until after burying his father, but Jesus said, "Follow Me." Why does God want us to prioritize doing His will over doing what we want to do?

_____
_____
_____
_____
_____
_____

➢ What kind(s) of circumstances make you fearful? How would your fears change, if Jesus was visibly with you, and you had unwavering faith that He is the Son of God?

_____
_____
_____
_____
_____
_____

➢ Why do you think demons recognize Jesus as the Son of God while many people do not?

_____
_____
_____
_____
_____
_____

## ACTION ITEM:

Exercise your faith. Confidently pray for God to help you or a loved one with a health or wellness issue.

## WHAT'S NEXT?

In the next chapter, Jesus links faith to healing again. As another person believes, it is done. Take note of Jesus' repeated words about having faith. Consider how your level of confidence in Jesus' ability to help you with your needs might be affecting the answers to your prayers. Remember, you can pray for more faith too!

# MATTHEW 9

He entered into a boat, and crossed over, and came into his own city. Behold, they brought to him a man who was paralyzed, lying on a bed. Jesus, seeing their faith, said to the paralytic, *"Son, cheer up! Your sins are forgiven you."*

Behold, some of the scribes said to themselves, "This man blasphemes."

Jesus, knowing their thoughts, said, *"Why do you think evil in your hearts? For which is easier, to say, 'Your sins are forgiven;' or to say, 'Get up, and walk?' But that you may know that the Son of Man has authority on earth to forgive sins"* (then he said to the paralytic), *"Get up, and take up your mat, and go to your house."*

He arose and departed to his house. But when the multitudes saw it, they marveled and glorified God, who had given such authority to men.

As Jesus passed by from there, he saw a man called Matthew sitting at the tax collection office. He said to him, *"Follow me."* He got up and followed him. As he sat in the house, behold, many tax collectors and sinners came and sat down with Jesus and his disciples. When the Pharisees saw it, they said to his disciples,

"Why does your teacher eat with tax collectors and sinners?"

When Jesus heard it, he said to them, *"Those who are healthy have no need for a physician, but those who are sick do. But you go and learn what this means: 'I desire mercy, and not sacrifice,' for I came not to call the righteous, but sinners to repentance."*

Then John's disciples came to him, saying, "Why do we and the Pharisees fast often, but your disciples don't fast?"

Jesus said to them, *"Can the friends of the bridegroom mourn, as long as the bridegroom is with them? But the days will come when the bridegroom will be taken away from them, and then they will fast. No one puts a piece of unshrunk cloth on an old garment; for the patch would tear away from the garment, and a worse hole is made. Neither do people put new wine into old wine skins, or else the skins would burst, and the wine be spilled, and the skins ruined. No, they put new wine into fresh wine skins, and both are preserved."*

While he told these things to them, behold, a ruler came and worshiped him, saying, "My daughter has just died, but come and lay your hand on her, and she will live."

Jesus got up and followed him, as did his disciples. Behold, a woman who had a discharge of blood for twelve years came behind him, and touched the fringe of his garment; for she said within herself, "If I just touch his garment, I will be made well."

But Jesus, turning around and seeing her, said, *"Daughter, cheer up! Your faith has made you well."* And the woman was made well from that hour.

When Jesus came into the ruler's house, and saw the flute players, and the crowd in noisy disorder, he said to them, *"Make room, because the girl isn't dead, but sleeping."*

They were ridiculing him. But when the crowd was put out, he entered in, took her by the hand, and the girl arose. The report of this went out into all that land.

As Jesus passed by from there, two blind men followed him, calling out and saying, "Have mercy on us, son of David!"

When he had come into the house, the blind men came to him. Jesus said to them, *"Do you believe that I am able to do this?"*

They told him, "Yes, Lord."

Then he touched their eyes, saying, *"According to your faith be it done to you."* Their eyes were opened. Jesus strictly commanded them, saying, *"See that no one knows about this."*

But they went out and spread abroad his fame in all that land.

As they went out, behold, a mute man who was demon possessed was brought to him. When the demon was cast out, the mute man spoke. The multitudes marveled, saying, "Nothing like this has ever been seen in Israel!"

But the Pharisees said, "By the prince of the demons, he casts out demons."

Jesus went about all the cities and the villages, teaching in their synagogues, and preaching the Good News of the Kingdom, and healing every disease and every sickness among the people. But when he saw the multitudes, he was moved with compassion for them, because they were harassed and scattered, like sheep without a shepherd. Then he said to his disciples, *"The harvest indeed is plentiful, but the laborers are few. Pray therefore that the Lord of the harvest will send out laborers into his harvest."*

# PROPHECIES IN THIS CHAPTER

**Daniel 7:14** – "There was given him dominion, and glory, and a kingdom, that all the peoples, nations, and languages should serve him: his dominion is an everlasting dominion, which shall not pass away, and his kingdom that which shall not be destroyed."

**Numbers 27:17** – "Who may go out before them, and who may come in before them, and who may lead them out, and who may bring them in; that the congregation of The Lord will not be as sheep which have no shepherd."

**1 Kings 22:17** – He said, "I saw all Israel scattered on the mountains, as sheep that have no shepherd. The Lord said, 'These have no master. Let them each return to his house in peace.'"

## WHY THESE PROPHECIES ARE IMPORTANT

In Matthew chapter 9, we see Jesus exercise His dominion over things on earth. The prophecy in Daniel 7:14 tells us that the Messiah will be given dominion and His Dominion will be an everlasting dominion.

At the beginning of Matthew, the scribes thought Jesus was blaspheming by telling a person his sins were forgiven. But Jesus demonstrated he has authority and dominion on Earth by telling the paralytic, "Get up, and take up your mat, and go to your house." The paralytic was able to do exactly that, which was far more difficult than forgiving the paralytic of his sins.

The remaining two prophecies in Numbers 27 and 1 Kings 22 both deal with the Israelites being as sheep without a shepherd. At the end of Matthew 9, Jesus is moved by compassion because the people are scattered like sheep without a shepherd. This is an important prophecy because upcoming prophecies speak of the Messiah as a shepherd of scattered sheep.

## WHAT STANDS OUT IN THESE PROPHECIES TO YOU?

## WHAT DO YOU THINK?

➢ Why do some people think evil thoughts toward Jesus, especially the religious leaders in this chapter?

➤ If Jesus leads us in the path of righteousness, and He wants tax collectors and sinners of all kinds to follow Him, why do you think many people refuse to even consider following Jesus?

___

➤ What do you think it means when Jesus says, I desire mercy and not sacrifice?

___

➤ Jesus came to call sinners to repentance. What sins did you list in chapters 5-7 for which you have not yet repented? Reflect on those and other sins in your life. Take time right now to repent.

___

➤ In the previous chapter (8) and twice in this one, Jesus indicates faith has resulted in a miracle. Based on your own level of faith, how likely or unlikely are miracles to occur in your life? What can you do to increase your faith?

___

➢ Why did the blind men call Jesus, "Son of David," when David lived 28 Generations earlier?

___
___
___
___
___
___
___

## ACTION ITEM:

List the miracles Jesus performed in this chapter:

___
___
___
___
___
___
___

Who do you know that needs a miracle? ___

Start praying for that person's miracle. Stretch your faith by asking others to join you in praying for the miracle.

## WHAT'S NEXT?

In the next chapter, Jesus talks about what it is like to serve God and the Kingdom of Heaven. He sends out His disciples to visit neighboring cities, and gives His disciples instructions for their journeys.

Take notice of Jesus' instructions to His disciples. Think about how His instructions might apply to your life as a Christian today.

What would you do or say if Jesus were here today, and He sent you out to talk to people about Him? Also consider what Jesus means when He talks about finding your life versus losing your life.

# MATTHEW 10

He called to himself his twelve disciples, and gave them authority over unclean spirits, to cast them out, and to heal every disease and every sickness. Now the names of the twelve apostles are these. The first, Simon, who is called Peter; Andrew, his brother; James the son of Zebedee; John, his brother; Philip; Bartholomew; Thomas; Matthew the tax collector; James the son of Alphaeus; Lebbaeus, who was also called Thaddaeus; Simon the Zealot; and Judas Iscariot, who also betrayed him.

Jesus sent these twelve out, and commanded them, saying, *"Don't go among the Gentiles, and don't enter into any city of the Samaritans. Rather, go to the lost sheep of the house of Israel. As you go, preach, saying, 'The Kingdom of Heaven is at hand!' Heal the sick, cleanse the lepers, and cast out demons. Freely you received, so freely give. Don't take any gold, silver, or brass in your money belts. Take no bag for your journey, neither two coats, nor sandals, nor staff: for the laborer is worthy of his food. Into whatever city or village you enter, find out who in it is worthy; and stay there until you go on. As you enter into the household, greet it.*

*"If the household is worthy, let your peace come on it, but if it isn't worthy, let your peace return to you.*

"Whoever doesn't receive you, nor hear your words, as you go out of that house or that city, shake the dust off your feet.

"Most certainly I tell you, it will be more tolerable for the land of Sodom and Gomorrah in the day of judgment than for that city.

"Behold, I send you out as sheep among wolves. Therefore be wise as serpents, and harmless as doves. But beware of men: for they will deliver you up to councils, and in their synagogues they will scourge you. Yes, and you will be brought before governors and kings for my sake, for a testimony to them and to the nations. But when they deliver you up, don't be anxious how or what you will say, for it will be given you in that hour what you will say. For it is not you who speak, but the Spirit of your Father who speaks in you.

"Brother will deliver up brother to death, and the father his child. Children will rise up against parents, and cause them to be put to death. You will be hated by all men for my name's sake, but he who endures to the end will be saved. But when they persecute you in this city, flee into the next, for most certainly I tell you, you will not have gone through the cities of Israel until the Son of Man has come.

"A disciple is not above his teacher, nor a servant above his lord. It is enough for the disciple that he be like his teacher, and the servant like his lord. If they have called the master of the house Beelzebul, how much more those of his household!

"Therefore don't be afraid of them, for there is nothing covered that will not be revealed; and hidden that will not be known. What I tell you in the darkness, speak in the light; and what you hear whispered in the ear, proclaim on the housetops. Don't be afraid of those who kill the body, but are not able to kill the soul. Rather, fear him who is able to destroy both soul and body in Gehenna.

"Aren't two sparrows sold for an assarion coin? Not one of them falls on the ground apart from your Father's will, but the very hairs of your head are all numbered.

"Therefore don't be afraid. You are of more value than many sparrows. Everyone therefore who confesses me before men, I will also confess him before my Father who is in heaven.

*"But whoever denies me before men, I will also deny him before my Father who is in heaven.*

*"Don't think that I came to send peace on the earth. I didn't come to send peace, but a sword. For I came to set a man at odds against his father, and a daughter against her mother, and a daughter-in-law against her mother-in-law. A man's foes will be those of his own household. He who loves father or mother more than me is not worthy of me; and he who loves son or daughter more than me isn't worthy of me. He who doesn't take his cross and follow after me, isn't worthy of me.*

*"He who seeks his life will lose it; and he who loses his life for my sake will find it. He who receives you receives me, and he who receives me receives him who sent me. He who receives a prophet in the name of a prophet will receive a prophet's reward. He who receives a righteous man in the name of a righteous man will receive a righteous man's reward. Whoever gives one of these little ones just a cup of cold water to drink in the name of a disciple, most certainly I tell you he will in no way lose his reward."*

## PROPHECIES IN THIS CHAPTER

**Deuteronomy 18:18** – I will raise them up a prophet from among their brothers, like you. I will put my words in his mouth, and he shall speak to them all that I shall command him.

**Matthew 10:17-18** - "But beware of men: for they will deliver you up to councils, and in their synagogues they will scourge you. Yes, and you will be brought before governors and kings for my sake, for a testimony to them and to the nations."

**Matthew 10:21-22** - "Brother will deliver up brother to death, and the father his child. Children will rise up against parents, and cause them to be put to death. You will be hated by all men for my name's sake, but he who endures to the end will be saved."

## WHY THESE PROPHECIES ARE IMPORTANT

In Matthew chapter 10, Jesus prophecies about how His disciples and followers will be treated by the men of the world. Jesus plainly tells His disciples they will be delivered up and brought before Governors and kings, and they will be hated because they follow Jesus. We know for a fact this prophecy came true, and even today it is true in many regions of the world.

As it relates to the Old Testament, Deuteronomy tells us the Messiah will be a prophet who will come up from among the brothers of Israel. As a descendant of David, Jesus is one of the brothers, and in chapter 10 we see Jesus speaking as a prophet. Jesus tells Prophecies of his own. He tells the disciples what will happen and what to expect. In this chapter in particular, Jesus is speaking as a prophet of God to God's people.

# WHAT STANDS OUT IN THESE PROPHECIES TO YOU?

_____
_____
_____
_____
_____
_____

# WHAT DO YOU THINK?

➤ John and Jesus said, "Repent, for the Kingdom of Heaven is at hand!" Now Jesus tells His disciples to declare the same. What does "the Kingdom of Heaven is at hand" mean, and how is it a warning?

_____
_____
_____
_____
_____
_____
_____
_____

➤ The disciples freely received Jesus's message of Salvation and authority to heal, so they are to freely share with others. What have you freely received which you can share with others?

_____
_____
_____
_____
_____
_____

➤ If you were brought before a council, governor, or king to give a testimony about Jesus, what would you say?

_____
_____
_____
_____
_____
_____

➢ Why are many people today more afraid of evil men than they are of God, when God has the ability to condemn them to hell?

_____
_____
_____
_____
_____
_____
_____
_____

➢ Jesus said he didn't come to bring peace, but He brought a sword. How is Jesus's sword of division evidenced in the world today?

_____
_____
_____
_____
_____
_____
_____
_____

➢ What does it look like when a person takes up his cross to follow Jesus? Have you taken up your cross? Why or why not?

_____
_____
_____
_____
_____
_____
_____

# ACTION ITEM:

When it comes to taking up your cross and following Jesus, what do you see yourself doing? What are some ways you can give of your time and/or talents to further God's Kingdom? Pray about how you can show God's love to someone outside your family in the next week. What will you do? Follow through with your plan.

_____
_____
_____
_____
_____
_____
_____
_____
_____

# WHAT'S NEXT?

In the next chapter, Jesus explains who is John the Baptist. As you read, think about why many people didn't recognize John the Baptist as the one who fulfilled the prophecies about one crying out in the wilderness and preparing the way for the Lord.

Think about how people's spiritual blindness in the first century is similar to people's spiritual blindness today.

Jesus also issues a couple of laments or "woes" to cities that existed in the first century. As you read, consider whether the "woes" could be directed at cities in today's world. What, if anything, is different in today's world, as compared to the first century, when it comes to understanding who is Jesus.

# MATTHEW 11

When Jesus had finished directing his twelve disciples, he departed from there to teach and preach in their cities. Now when John heard in the prison the works of Christ, he sent two of his disciples and said to him, "Are you he who comes, or should we look for another?"

Jesus answered them, *"Go and tell John the things which you hear and see: the blind receive their sight, the lame walk, the lepers are cleansed, the deaf hear, the dead are raised up, and the poor have good news preached to them. Blessed is he who finds no occasion for stumbling in me."*

As these went their way, Jesus began to say to the multitudes concerning John, *"What did you go out into the wilderness to see? A reed shaken by the wind? But what did you go out to see? A man in soft clothing? Behold, those who wear soft clothing are in kings' houses. But why did you go out? To see a prophet? Yes, I tell you, and much more than a prophet. For this is he, of whom it is written, 'Behold, I send my messenger before your face, who will prepare your way before you.'*

*"Most certainly I tell you, among those who are born of women there has not arisen anyone greater than John the Baptizer; yet he who is least in the Kingdom of Heaven is greater than he.*

*"From the days of John the Baptizer until now, the Kingdom of Heaven suffers violence, and the violent take it by force. For all the prophets and the law prophesied until John. If you are willing to receive it, this is Elijah, who is to come. He who has ears to hear, let him hear.*

*"But to what shall I compare this generation? It is like children sitting in the marketplaces, who call to their companions and say, 'We played the flute for you, and you didn't dance. We mourned for you, and you didn't lament.' For John came neither eating nor drinking, and they say, 'He has a demon.' The Son of Man came eating and drinking, and they say, 'Behold, a gluttonous man and a drunkard, a friend of tax collectors and sinners!' But wisdom is justified by her children."*

Then he began to denounce the cities in which most of his mighty works had been done, because they didn't repent.

*"Woe to you, Chorazin! Woe to you, Bethsaida! For if the mighty works had been done in Tyre and Sidon which were done in you, they would have repented long ago in sackcloth and ashes. But I tell you, it will be more tolerable for Tyre and Sidon on the day of judgment than for you.*

*"You, Capernaum, who are exalted to heaven, you will go down to Hades. For if the mighty works had been done in Sodom which were done in you, it would have remained until today. But I tell you that it will be more tolerable for the land of Sodom, on the day of judgment, than for you."*

At that time, Jesus answered, *"I thank you, Father, Lord of heaven and earth, that you hid these things from the wise and understanding, and revealed them to infants. Yes, Father, for so it was well-pleasing in your sight. All things have been delivered to me by my Father. No one knows the Son, except the Father; neither does anyone know the Father, except the Son, and he to whom the Son desires to reveal him.*

*"Come to me, all you who labor and are heavily burdened, and I will give you rest. Take my yoke upon you, and learn from me, for I am gentle and humble in heart; and you will find rest for your souls. For my yoke is easy, and my burden is light."*

# PROPHECIES IN THIS CHAPTER

**Isaiah 35:5-6** – "Then the eyes of the blind will be opened, and the ears of the deaf will be unstopped. Then the lame man will leap like a deer, and the tongue of the mute will sing; for waters will break out in the wilderness, and streams in the desert."

**Malachi 3:1** – "Behold, I send my messenger, and he will prepare the way before me; and the Lord, whom you seek, will suddenly come to his temple; and the messenger of the covenant, whom you desire, behold, he comes!" says the Lord of Armies."

**Malachi 4:5-6** – "Behold, I will send you Elijah the prophet before the great and terrible day of the Lord comes. He will turn the hearts of the fathers to the children, and the hearts of the children to their fathers, lest I come and strike the earth with a curse."

**Isaiah 8:14** – He will be a sanctuary, but for both houses of Israel, he will be a trap and a snare for the inhabitants of Jerusalem.

**Isaiah 1:4** – Ah sinful nation, a people loaded with iniquity, offspring of evildoers, children who deal corruptly! They have forsaken The Lord. They have despised the Holy One of Israel. They are estranged and backward.

**Zechariah 9:9** – Rejoice greatly, daughter of Zion! Shout, daughter of Jerusalem!

Behold, your King comes to you! He is righteous, and having salvation; lowly, and riding on a donkey, even on a colt, the foal of a donkey.

# WHY THESE PROPHECIES ARE IMPORTANT

The prophecies from Malachi reiterate the fact that the Messiah will be preceded by a messenger. Some of the old scriptures say that Elijah will come before the Messiah, and in this chapter of Matthew, Jesus plainly tells us John the Baptist is Elijah, who was prophesied to come before him. This is a reinforcement of some of the prophecies we saw earlier in the Book of Matthew regarding John the Baptist as the messenger and voice crying out in the wilderness.

From Isaiah, we see the Messiah will open the eyes of the blind, open the ears of the deaf, and help lame man walk again. Since Jesus performed these Miracles, He easily fulfills this prophecy.

We also see in Isaiah, the Messiah will be a trap and a snare for Israel and Jerusalem, but He will be a sanctuary for other people. This goes right along with many people believing Jesus is the Messiah, but the leaders of the Jewish faith do not see Jesus as the Messiah. They are blinded by their own thinking.

These prophecies are particularly important, regarding the Jewish people rejecting Jesus, because that is how history has played out. Jewish people are still blind to their own prophecies, as they relate to Jesus. They are still expecting a Messiah that fits their vision for a leader, which they believe will be someone who is a warrior who will defeat all of their enemies on earth.

However, the scriptures say the King of the Jews will come as one who is humble. The verse from Zechariah specifically prophecies the coming events where Jesus rides into Jerusalem on a donkey. In this chapter, it's important to note the Messiah has a lowly disposition. The ancient prophecies make it clear, the Messiah is not going to be valiant warrior riding into town on a magnificent steed! The scriptures say He'll be lowly and riding on a donkey.

# WHAT STANDS OUT IN THESE PROPHECIES TO YOU?

# WHAT DO YOU THINK?

➢ John the Baptist baptized Jesus, saw the spirit of God descend on Jesus, and John heard God speak from Heaven. Why do you think John is now wondering if Jesus is the Messiah?

➢ So far, what convinces you the most that Jesus is the one which ancient prophecy said would come? What doubts, if any, do you have?

➢ Why did people go out to the wilderness to see John? Why are multitudes coming to see Jesus? What do you think people are seeking, which they don't already have?

➢ In what ways does the Kingdom of Heaven suffer violence on Earth today?

___

➢ What makes people reject both John the Baptist (who didn't dine with sinners), and Jesus (who dined with sinners and drank wine)? Why can't they see God's truth in either one of them?

___

➢ In your life, what makes you feel burdened? What would rest for your soul look like?

___

# ACTION ITEM:

Jesus tells us to learn from Him to find rest for our souls. The fastest way to learn what Jesus taught is by reading the four Gospels (Matthew, Mark, Luke, and John). If you haven't read all four Gospels yet, make a commitment to read them when you finish this study. Go ahead and schedule Gospel reading into your calendar, so you won't forget to read them. If you read one chapter per day, it will take about three months to read all of the Gospels, because there are 89 chapters total in the Gospels.

# WHAT'S NEXT?

In the next chapter, the Pharisees (church leaders) begin to question Jesus' actions and they wonder who is He. Look for the wisdom in Jesus' responses to the Pharisees. Look for important truths you can take away from Jesus' teachings, and consider how you can apply them to your life.

Pay close attention to Jesus' teaching about divided kingdoms. Think about how His teaching relates to divided households, families, and societies today.

# MATTHEW 12

At that time, Jesus went on the Sabbath day through the grain fields. His disciples were hungry and began to pluck heads of grain and to eat. But the Pharisees, when they saw it, said to him, "Behold, your disciples do what is not lawful to do on the Sabbath."

But he said to them, *"Haven't you read what David did, when he was hungry, and those who were with him; how he entered into God's house, and ate the show bread, which was not lawful for him to eat, neither for those who were with him, but only for the priests? Or have you not read in the law, that on the Sabbath day, the priests in the temple profane the Sabbath, and are guiltless? But I tell you that one greater than the temple is here. But if you had known what this means, 'I desire mercy, and not sacrifice,' you wouldn't have condemned the guiltless. For the Son of Man is Lord of the Sabbath."*

He departed from there, and went into their synagogue. And behold there was a man with a withered hand. They asked him, "Is it lawful to heal on the Sabbath day?" that they might accuse him.

He said to them, *"What man is there among you, who has one sheep, and if this one falls into a pit on the Sabbath day, won't he grab on to it, and lift it out?*

*Of how much more value is a man than a sheep! Therefore it is lawful to do good on the Sabbath day."*

Then he told the man, *"Stretch out your hand."* He stretched it out; and it was restored whole, just like the other. But the Pharisees went out, and conspired against him, how they might destroy him. Jesus, perceiving that, withdrew from there. Great multitudes followed him; and he healed them all, and commanded them that they should not make him known: that it might be fulfilled which was spoken through Isaiah the prophet, saying:

"Behold, my servant whom I have chosen; my beloved in whom my soul is well pleased: I will put my Spirit on him.

"He will proclaim justice to the nations.

"He will not strive, nor shout; neither will anyone hear his voice in the streets.

"He won't break a bruised reed.

"He won't quench a smoking flax, until he leads justice to victory.

"In his name, the nations will hope."

Then one possessed by a demon, blind and mute, was brought to him and he healed him, so that the blind and mute man both spoke and saw. All the multitudes were amazed, and said, "Can this be the son of David?" But when the Pharisees heard it, they said, "This man does not cast out demons, except by Beelzebul, the prince of the demons."

Knowing their thoughts, Jesus said to them, *"Every kingdom divided against itself is brought to desolation, and every city or house divided against itself will not stand. If Satan casts out Satan, he is divided against himself. How then will his kingdom stand? If I by Beelzebul cast out demons, by whom do your children cast them out? Therefore they will be your judges. But if I by the Spirit of God cast out demons, then God's Kingdom has come upon you.*

*"Or how can one enter into the house of the strong man, and plunder his goods, unless he first bind the strong man? Then he will plunder his house.*

"He who is not with me is against me, and he who doesn't gather with me, scatters. Therefore I tell you, every sin and blasphemy will be forgiven men, but the blasphemy against the Spirit will not be forgiven men. Whoever speaks a word against the Son of Man, it will be forgiven him; but whoever speaks against the Holy Spirit, it will not be forgiven him, neither in this age, nor in that which is to come.

"Either make the tree good, and its fruit good, or make the tree corrupt, and its fruit corrupt; for the tree is known by its fruit. You offspring of vipers, how can you, being evil, speak good things? For out of the abundance of the heart, the mouth speaks. The good man out of his good treasure brings out good things, and the evil man out of his evil treasure brings out evil things. I tell you that every idle word that men speak, they will give account of it in the day of judgment. For by your words you will be justified, and by your words you will be condemned."

Then certain of the scribes and Pharisees answered, "Teacher, we want to see a sign from you."

But he answered them, "*An evil and adulterous generation seeks after a sign, but no sign will be given to it but the sign of Jonah the prophet. For as Jonah was three days and three nights in the belly of the whale, so will the Son of Man be three days and three nights in the heart of the earth. The men of Nineveh will stand up in the judgment with this generation, and will condemn it, for they repented at the preaching of Jonah; and behold, someone greater than Jonah is here.*

"*The Queen of the South will rise up in the judgment with this generation, and will condemn it, for she came from the ends of the earth to hear the wisdom of Solomon; and behold, someone greater than Solomon is here.*

"*When an unclean spirit has gone out of a man, he passes through waterless places, seeking rest, and doesn't find it. Then he says, 'I will return into my house from which I came out,' and when he has come back, he finds it empty, swept, and put in order. Then he goes, and takes with himself seven other spirits more evil than he is, and they enter in and dwell there. The last state of that man becomes worse than the first. Even so will it be also to this evil generation.*"

While he was yet speaking to the multitudes, behold, his mother and his brothers stood outside, seeking to speak to him. One said to him, "Behold, your mother and your brothers stand outside, seeking to speak to you." But he answered him who spoke to him, *"Who is my mother? Who are my brothers?"*

He stretched out his hand toward his disciples, and said, *"Behold, my mother and my brothers! For whoever does the will of my Father who is in heaven, he is my brother, and sister, and mother."*

## PROPHECIES IN THIS CHAPTER

**Daniel 7:13-14** – "I saw in the night visions, and behold, there came with the clouds of the sky one like a son of man, and he came even to the ancient of days, and they brought him near before him. There was given him dominion, and glory, and a kingdom, that all the peoples, nations, and languages should serve him: his dominion is an everlasting dominion, which shall not pass away, and his kingdom that which shall not be destroyed."

**Isaiah 61:1** – The Lord God's Spirit is on me; because The Lord has anointed me to preach good news to the humble. He has sent me to bind up the broken hearted, to proclaim liberty to the captives, and release to those who are bound;

**Isaiah 42:1-7** –
1 "Behold, my servant, whom I uphold; my chosen, in whom my soul delights—
I have put my Spirit on him. He will bring justice to the nations.
2 He will not shout, nor raise his voice, nor cause it to be heard in the street.
3 He won't break a bruised reed.
He won't quench a dimly burning wick.
He will faithfully bring justice.
4 He will not fail nor be discouraged, until he has set justice in the earth, and the islands will wait for his law."
5 Thus says God The Lord, he who created the heavens and stretched them out,
he who spread out the earth and that which comes out of it,
he who gives breath to its people and spirit to those who walk in it.
6 "I, The Lord, have called you in righteousness, and will hold your hand, and will keep you,
and make you a covenant for the people, as a light for the nations;
7 to open the blind eyes, to bring the prisoners out of the dungeon, and those who sit in darkness out of the prison.

**Jonah 1:17** – "The Lord prepared a great fish to swallow up Jonah, and Jonah was in the belly of the fish three days and three nights."

**Matthew 12:40** – "For as Jonah was three days and three nights in the belly of the whale, so will the Son of Man be three days and three nights in the heart of the earth."

# WHY THESE PROPHECIES ARE IMPORTANT

Here in Chapter 12, Daniel 7:14 is referenced again, which prophesied the dominion of the Messiah over all things. In Matthew 12, Jesus says He is Lord of the Sabbath, which is just one of the many things over which He has Dominion. This prophecy is referenced by many versions of the Bible at different points in the Book of Matthew. So, it is not a mistake that it reappears here. For some of the repeated prophecy references later in this book, I will refer you to a prior chapter where it appeared, rather than writing the verses and explanations out again for you.

The prophecy in Isaiah 61 speaks to the messiah's anointing by God and the placing of God's spirit within him. For all who knew Jesus, it was evident that God's Spirit was with Him, because He spoke with unexpected wisdom. He also proclaimed liberty and release, just as this prophecy predicted the Messiah would do.

Isaiah 42 is a lengthier Passage that describes the Messiah in more detail. If you read through Isaiah 42 with Jesus in mind, you should be able to see many of the characteristics of the Messiah fit Jesus. These long passages of description are particularly important, because they let us know the character and the actions of the Messiah. When we see how well the descriptions fits Jesus, it makes it easier to believe Jesus is the fulfillment of these ancient prophecies

The prophecy from Jonah is more obscure. It would be difficult, in a brief synopsis like this, to explain how Jonah spending three days and three nights in the belly of a whale is really a prophecy about Jesus. If you want to fully understand the concept behind this prophecy, I'd recommend Timothy Keller's book called, The Prodigal Prophet, as a reference. Otherwise, suffice it to say, Jesus refers to the story of Jonah and the whale as a sign about the Messiah. In this context, Jesus prophesies that He will be crucified and dead for the same length of time Jonah was in the belly of the whale. It is a sign for the Jewish people from their ancient scriptures, if they choose to believe it.

# WHAT STANDS OUT IN THESE PROPHECIES TO YOU?

_____
_____
_____
_____
_____
_____
_____
_____
_____
_____
_____
_____

# WHAT DO YOU THINK?

➤ Since the Sabbath is a day of rest unto the Lord, and it is okay to do good on the Sabbath, what sorts of things do you think would be improper to do on the Sabbath?

_____
_____
_____
_____
_____
_____

➤ What do you think it looks like for you to rest unto the Lord?

_____
_____
_____
_____
_____
_____

➤ The phrase, "I desire mercy, and not sacrifice," first appears in the Old Testament book of Hosea 6:6, and now twice in the book of Matthew. What does it look like to give other people mercy?

_____
_____
_____
_____

➤ When you speak, what do your words typically reveal about your heart?

_____
_____
_____
_____
_____

➢ Why do people continually desire signs from God, rather than believe what God already said in His Word, the Bible? Why don't people believe the documented history written in the Bible?

___

➢ What habits can you adopt to ensure your spirit stays connected with God?

___

# ACTION ITEM:

From the six questions above, pick one area of self-improvement to focus on. Consider how you typically:

- Spend your Sabbath day,
- Rest in the Lord,
- Offer mercy versus sacrifice,
- How you speak to others or about others,
- Your strength of faith, and
- Your spiritual habits.

Which of these areas needs the most work to bring you closer to God's holiness? Write a brief prayer for improvement in that area. Begin to pray daily for God to change your heart and your actions.

# WHAT'S NEXT?

In the next chapter, Jesus begins teaching in parables. Without the Holy Spirit's help, it can be difficult to understand Jesus' teachings when they are presented as parables.

Therefore, in the upcoming chapters, if you have difficulty understanding what Jesus is talking about, ask the Holy Spirit to give you understanding. That's why the Holy Spirit is with us—to help us!

In the next chapter, Jesus teaches what the Kingdom of Heaven is like. Focus on the examples Jesus gives. Reread as needed to understand what the Kingdom of Heaven is really like and to understand how the Kingdom grows.

# MATTHEW 13

On that day Jesus went out of the house, and sat by the seaside. Great multitudes gathered to him, so that he entered into a boat, and sat, and all the multitude stood on the beach. He spoke to them many things in parables, saying, *"Behold, a farmer went out to sow. As he sowed, some seeds fell by the roadside, and the birds came and devoured them. Others fell on rocky ground, where they didn't have much soil, and immediately they sprang up, because they had no depth of earth. When the sun had risen, they were scorched. Because they had no root, they withered away. Others fell among thorns. The thorns grew up and choked them. Others fell on good soil, and yielded fruit: some one hundred times as much, some sixty, and some thirty. He who has ears to hear, let him hear."*

The disciples came, and said to him, "Why do you speak to them in parables?"

He answered them, *"To you it is given to know the mysteries of the Kingdom of Heaven, but it is not given to them. For whoever has, to him will be given, and he will have abundance, but whoever doesn't have, from him will be taken away even that which he has. Therefore I speak to them in parables, because seeing they don't see, and hearing, they don't hear, neither do they understand. In them the prophecy of Isaiah is fulfilled, which says, 'By hearing you will hear, and will in no way understand; Seeing you will see, and will in no way perceive: for this people's heart has grown callous, their ears are dull of hearing, they have closed their eyes; or else perhaps they might perceive with their eyes, hear with their ears, understand with their heart, and would turn again; and I would heal them.'*

"But blessed are your eyes, for they see; and your ears, for they hear. For most certainly I tell you that many prophets and righteous men desired to see the things which you see, and didn't see them; and to hear the things which you hear, and didn't hear them.

"Hear, then, the parable of the farmer. When anyone hears the word of the Kingdom, and doesn't understand it, the evil one comes, and snatches away that which has been sown in his heart. This is what was sown by the roadside. What was sown on the rocky places, this is he who hears the word, and immediately with joy receives it; yet he has no root in himself, but endures for a while. When oppression or persecution arises because of the word, immediately he stumbles. What was sown among the thorns, this is he who hears the word, but the cares of this age and the deceitfulness of riches choke the word, and he becomes unfruitful.

"What was sown on the good ground, this is he who hears the word, and understands it, who most certainly bears fruit, and produces, some one hundred times as much, some sixty, and some thirty."

He set another parable before them, saying,

"The Kingdom of Heaven is like a man who sowed good seed in his field, but while people slept, his enemy came and sowed darnel weeds also among the wheat, and went away. But when the blade sprang up and produced fruit, then the darnel weeds appeared also. The servants of the householder came and said to him, 'Sir, didn't you sow good seed in your field? Where did these darnel weeds come from?'

"He said to them, 'An enemy has done this.'

"The servants asked him, 'Do you want us to go and gather them up?'

"But he said, 'No, lest perhaps while you gather up the darnel weeds, you root up the wheat with them. Let both grow together until the harvest, and in the harvest *time I will tell the reapers, "First, gather up the darnel weeds, and bind them in bundles to burn them; but gather the wheat into my barn."*

He set another parable before them, saying,

*"The Kingdom of Heaven is like a grain of mustard seed, which a man took, and sowed in his field; which indeed is smaller than all seeds. But when it is grown, it is greater than the herbs, and becomes a tree, so that the birds of the air come and lodge in its branches."*

He spoke another parable to them. *"The Kingdom of Heaven is like yeast, which a woman took, and hid in three measures of meal, until it was all leavened."*

Jesus spoke all these things in parables to the multitudes; and without a parable, he didn't speak to them, that it might be fulfilled which was spoken through the prophet, saying,

*"I will open my mouth in parables; I will utter things hidden from the foundation of the world."*

Then Jesus sent the multitudes away, and went into the house. His disciples came to him, saying, "Explain to us the parable of the darnel weeds of the field."

He answered them, *"He who sows the good seed is the Son of Man, the field is the world; and the good seed, these are the children of the Kingdom; and the darnel weeds are the children of the evil one. The enemy who sowed them is the devil. The harvest is the end of the age, and the reapers are angels. As therefore the darnel weeds are gathered up and burned with fire; so will it be at the end of this age."*

*"The Son of Man will send out his angels, and they will gather out of his Kingdom all things that cause stumbling, and those who do iniquity, and will cast them into the furnace of fire. There will be the weeping and the gnashing of teeth.*

*"Then the righteous will shine like the sun in the Kingdom of their Father. He who has ears to hear, let him hear.*

*"Again, the Kingdom of Heaven is like treasure hidden in the field, which a man found, and hid.*

*"In his joy, he goes and sells all that he has, and buys that field.*

"Again, the Kingdom of Heaven is like a man who is a merchant seeking fine pearls, who having found one pearl of great price, he went and sold all that he had, and bought it.

"Again, the Kingdom of Heaven is like a dragnet, that was cast into the sea, and gathered some fish of every kind, which, when it was filled, they drew up on the beach. They sat down, and gathered the good into containers, but the bad they threw away.

"So will it be in the end of the world. The angels will come and separate the wicked from among the righteous, and will cast them into the furnace of fire. There will be the weeping and the gnashing of teeth."

Jesus said to them, "*Have you understood all these things?*"

They answered him, "Yes, Lord."

He said to them, "*Therefore every scribe who has been made a disciple in the Kingdom of Heaven is like a man who is a householder, who brings out of his treasure new and old things.*"

When Jesus had finished these parables, he departed from there. Coming into his own country, he taught them in their synagogue, so that they were astonished, and said, "Where did this man get this wisdom, and these mighty works? Isn't this the carpenter's son? Isn't his mother called Mary, and his brothers, James, Joses, Simon, and Judas? Aren't all of his sisters with us? Where then did this man get all of these things?" They were offended by him.

But Jesus said to them, "*A prophet is not without honor, except in his own country, and in his own house.*" He didn't do many mighty works there because of their unbelief.

# PROPHECIES IN THIS CHAPTER

**Daniel 7:13-14** – To read this prophecy again, see Chapters 9 & 12 in this book.

**Deuteronomy 18:15-19** – "The Lord your God will raise up to you a prophet from among you, of your brothers, like me. You shall listen to him. This is according to all that you desired of The Lord your God in Horeb in the day of the assembly, saying, 'Let me not hear again The Lord my God's voice, neither let me see this great fire any more, that I not die.'

"The Lord said to me, 'They have well said that which they have spoken. I will raise them up a prophet from among their brothers, like you. I will put my words in his mouth, and he shall speak to them all that I shall command him. It shall happen, that whoever will not listen to my words which he shall speak in my name, I will require it of him.'"

**Psalm 78:2** – I will open my mouth in a parable. I will utter dark sayings of old.

**Ezekiel 12:2** – Son of man, you dwell in the middle of the rebellious house, who have eyes to see, and don't see, who have ears to hear, and don't hear; for they are a rebellious house.

**Ezekiel 33:31-32** – They come to you as the people come, and they sit before you as my people, and they hear your words, but don't do them; for with their mouth they show much love, but their heart goes after their gain. Behold, you are to them as a very lovely song of one who has a pleasant voice, and can play well on an instrument; for they hear your words, but they don't do them.

## WHY THESE PROPHECIES ARE IMPORTANT

Many versions of the Bible reference Daniel 7:13-14 again, regarding God raising up a prophet from among the brothers and saying that we shall listen to him. You can refer back to chapters 9 & 12 for the explanation of the Daniel 7 prophecy, which we already covered.

One of the most specific prophecies comes from Psalm 78 to where it says the Messiah will open his mouth in parables and utter dark sayings of old. Jesus frequently teaches in parables, particularly in this chapter of Matthew. There aren't many people who teach in Parables, so this characteristic of Jesus makes him one of few people who match this particular description of the Messiah.

The prophecy in Ezekiel 12:2 says the Messiah will dwell with those who have eyes and ears, but they don't see or hear. Since the people aren't understanding Jesus, He is dwelling in the middle of them, as was prophesied. Ezekiel refers to the people of Israel, as the rebellious house too, which matches Jesus' description of them as a rebellious generation.

These prophecies regarding the blindness of Israel toward Jesus as the Messiah are crucial for understanding who will be the Messiah. He will not be somebody that Israel recognizes and says, "Oh, there's our Messiah!" They will recognize Jesus at His second coming, as will everyone in the world, but for this age, it is important to understand Israel's rejection of Jesus is exactly what was prophesied to happen. The fact that Israel rejects Jesus is an important indicator He is the Messiah!

## WHAT STANDS OUT IN THESE PROPHECIES TO YOU?

_____
_____
_____
_____
_____
_____
_____
_____

# WHAT DO YOU THINK?

➤ In the parable of sowing seeds, some people never connect with God. Some connect, but quickly disconnect or drift away. Others connect and remain with God, growing and flourishing. What behaviors and characteristics do you see in people who are growing in their relationship with God?

_____
_____
_____
_____
_____
_____
_____
_____
_____
_____

➤ What do you think makes people unable or unwilling to hear God's Word?

_____
_____
_____
_____
_____
_____
_____
_____
_____
_____

➤ What riches are you pursuing besides God?

_____
_____
_____
_____
_____
_____
_____
_____
_____
_____

➢ What cares of this age get in your way, and keep you from spending time with God and His Word? What can you do differently to make more time for God in your life?

___

➢ What has caused Jesus' influence to continually grow throughout the world? In other words, what do you think is the *hidden yeast* that continually causes Christianity to spread through the years?

___

➢ What would you say is the true value of the Kingdom of Heaven in your life?

___

## ACTION ITEM:

Pick the parable in this chapter which is the most difficult for you to understand. Research those Bible verses at BibleHub.com, so you will better understand what Jesus meant.

## WHAT'S NEXT?

There are three main events shared in the next chapter: Why Herod thinks Jesus is John the Baptist, Jesus' miracle of feeding 5000, and the famous incident where Jesus walks on water. As you read, think about these three story lines. Consider from which you gain the most meaningful insight(s).

# MATTHEW 14

At that time, Herod the tetrarch heard the report concerning Jesus, and said to his servants, "This is John the Baptizer. He is risen from the dead. That is why these powers work in him." For Herod had arrested John, and bound him, and put him in prison for the sake of Herodias, his brother Philip's wife. For John said to him, "It is not lawful for you to have her." When he would have put him to death, he feared the multitude, because they counted him as a prophet.

But when Herod's birthday came, the daughter of Herodias danced among them and pleased Herod. Whereupon he promised with an oath to give her whatever she should ask. She, being prompted by her mother, said, "Give me here on a platter the head of John the Baptizer."

The king was grieved, but for the sake of his oaths, and of those who sat at the table with him, he commanded it to be given, and he sent and beheaded John in the prison. His head was brought on a platter, and given to the young lady; and she brought it to her mother. His disciples came, and took the body, and buried it. Then they went and told Jesus.

Now when Jesus heard this, he withdrew from there in a boat, to a deserted place apart. When the multitudes heard it, they followed him on foot from the cities.

Jesus went out, and he saw a great multitude. He had compassion on them, and healed their sick. When evening had come, his disciples came to him, saying, "This place is deserted, and the hour is already late. Send the multitudes away, that they may go into the villages, and buy themselves food."

But Jesus said to them, *"They don't need to go away. You give them something to eat."*

They told him, "We only have here five loaves and two fish."

He said, *"Bring them here to me."* He commanded the multitudes to sit down on the grass; and he took the five loaves and the two fish, and looking up to heaven, he blessed, broke and gave the loaves to the disciples, and the disciples gave to the multitudes. They all ate, and were filled. They took up twelve baskets full of that which remained left over from the broken pieces. Those who ate were about five thousand men, in addition to women and children.

Immediately Jesus made the disciples get into the boat, and to go ahead of him to the other side, while he sent the multitudes away. After he had sent the multitudes away, he went up into the mountain by himself to pray. When evening had come, he was there alone. But the boat was now in the middle of the sea, distressed by the waves, for the wind was contrary. In the fourth watch of the night, Jesus came to them, walking on the sea. When the disciples saw him walking on the sea, they were troubled, saying, "It's a ghost!" and they cried out for fear. But immediately Jesus spoke to them, saying, *"Cheer up! It is I! Don't be afraid."*

Peter answered him and said, "Lord, if it is you, command me to come to you on the waters."

He said, *"Come!"*

Peter stepped down from the boat, and walked on the waters to come to Jesus. But when he saw that the wind was strong, he was afraid, and beginning to sink, he cried out, saying, "Lord, save me!"

Immediately Jesus stretched out his hand, took hold of him, and said to him, *"You of little faith, why did you doubt?"* When they got up into the boat, the wind ceased.

Those who were in the boat came and worshiped him, saying, "You are truly the Son of God!"

When they had crossed over, they came to the land of Gennesaret. When the people of that place recognized him, they sent into all that surrounding region, and brought to him all who were sick; and they begged him that they might just touch the fringe of his garment. As many as touched it were made whole.

## PROPHECIES IN THIS CHAPTER

**Isaiah 40:11** – "He will feed his flock like a shepherd.
He will gather the lambs in his arm, and carry them in his bosom.
He will gently lead those who have their young."

## WHY THIS PROPHECY IS IMPORTANT

In this prophecy from Isaiah, we see the Messiah will feed his flock like a Shepherd. In Matthew 14, Jesus feeds more than 5000 people through a miracle using five loaves of bread and two fish. This prophecy also says the Messiah will gather the lambs in his arms and carry them, and he will gently lead those who have their young. This passage figuratively speaks about how the Messiah will care for his people. Jesus' compassion for the crowd and His miracle feeding shows He is gentle with the people.

## WHAT STANDS OUT IN THIS PROPHECY TO YOU?

# WHAT DO YOU THINK?

➤ After Herod had John the Baptist beheaded, what would make Herod think Jesus was John the Baptist raised from the dead? What fears do you think Herod was experiencing?

___

➤ In the Old Testament prophecy of Isaiah 40:11 it says, the Messiah will feed his flock like a Shepherd. The miracle of feeding more than 5000+ with five loaves of bread and two fish shows Jesus fed the multitude. In what ways do the prophecy and the miracle of feeding 5000+ show the character and compassion of Christ being like a shepherd?

___

➤ Of what are you afraid, to which Jesus might tell you, "Cheer up! Don't Be Afraid?" What would give you hope and cheer you up in this fearful situation of yours?

___

➤ Peter walked on water until he lost his faith. What does this reveal to you about the nature of faith?

___

➤ Why do people have an abundance of doubt and relatively little faith when it comes to believing in God's ability to do anything?

___

➤ The disciples said, "You are truly the Son of God," when Jesus walked on water. Which of Jesus's miracles, teachings, or other acts compel you the most to believe Jesus truly is the son of God?

___

## ACTION ITEM:

Reread what Jesus does and says when Peter attempts to walk on the water. Did you notice Jesus reaches out to take Peter's hand first? Jesus wonders why Peter's faith is little, when Peter was just walking on water!

Go to BibleGateway.com or a similar tool, and search for the phrase "don't be afraid" in the Bible. Read over the verses, and pick one to memorize as your comfort verse for the next time your faith is wavering. Write your chosen verse here:

_____
_____
_____
_____
_____
_____
_____
_____

## WHAT'S NEXT?

In the next chapter you will experience three more interesting episodes with Jesus. The first is a teaching parable. The second involves a Canaanite woman whose daughter is possessed, and the third is a miracle of Jesus feeding 4,000. As with the previous chapter, as you read, think about these three incidents, and consider from which you gain the most meaningful insight.

# MATTHEW 15

Then Pharisees and scribes came to Jesus from Jerusalem, saying, "Why do your disciples disobey the tradition of the elders? For they don't wash their hands when they eat bread."

He answered them, *"Why do you also disobey the commandment of God because of your tradition? For God commanded, 'Honor your father and your mother,' and, 'He who speaks evil of father or mother, let him be put to death.' But you say, 'Whoever may tell his father or his mother, "Whatever help you might otherwise have gotten from me is a gift devoted to God," he shall not honor his father or mother.' You have made the commandment of God void because of your tradition.*

*"You hypocrites! Well did Isaiah prophesy of you, saying, 'These people draw near to me with their mouth, and honor me with their lips; but their heart is far from me. And in vain do they worship me, teaching as doctrine rules made by men.'"*

He summoned the multitude, and said to them, *"Hear, and understand. That which enters into the mouth doesn't defile the man; but that which proceeds out of the mouth, this defiles the man."*

Then the disciples came, and said to him, "Do you know that the Pharisees were offended when they heard this saying?"

But he answered, *"Every plant which my heavenly Father didn't plant will be uprooted. Leave them alone. They are blind guides of the blind. If the blind guide the blind, both will fall into a pit."*

Peter answered him, "Explain the parable to us."

So Jesus said, *"Do you also still not understand? Don't you understand that whatever goes into the mouth passes into the belly, and then out of the body? But the things which proceed out of the mouth come out of the heart, and they defile the man. For out of the heart come evil thoughts, murders, adulteries, sexual sins, thefts, false testimony, and blasphemies. These are the things which defile the man; but to eat with unwashed hands doesn't defile the man."*

Jesus went out from there, and withdrew into the region of Tyre and Sidon. Behold, a Canaanite woman came out from those borders, and cried, saying, "Have mercy on me, Lord, you son of David! My daughter is severely possessed by a demon!"

But he answered her not a word.

His disciples came and begged him, saying, "Send her away; for she cries after us."

But he answered, *"I wasn't sent to anyone but the lost sheep of the house of Israel."*

But she came and worshiped him, saying, "Lord, help me."

But he answered, *"It is not appropriate to take the children's bread and throw it to the dogs."*

But she said, "Yes, Lord, but even the dogs eat the crumbs which fall from their masters' table."

Then Jesus answered her, *"Woman, great is your faith! Be it done to you even as you desire."*

And her daughter was healed from that hour.

Jesus departed from there, and came near to the sea of Galilee; and he went up into the mountain, and sat there. Great multitudes came to him, having with them the lame, blind, mute, maimed, and many others, and they put them down at his feet.

He healed them, so that the multitude wondered when they saw the mute speaking, the injured healed, the lame walking, and the blind seeing—and they glorified the God of Israel.

Jesus summoned his disciples and said, *"I have compassion on the multitude, because they continue with me now three days and have nothing to eat. I don't want to send them away fasting, or they might faint on the way."*

The disciples said to him, "Where should we get so many loaves in a deserted place as to satisfy so great a multitude?"

Jesus said to them, *"How many loaves do you have?"*

They said, "Seven, and a few small fish."

He commanded the multitude to sit down on the ground; and he took the seven loaves and the fish. He gave thanks and broke them, and gave to the disciples, and the disciples to the multitudes. They all ate, and were filled. They took up seven baskets full of the broken pieces that were left over. Those who ate were four thousand men, in addition to women and children.

Then he sent away the multitudes, got into the boat, and came into the borders of Magdala.

# PROPHECIES IN THIS CHAPTER

**Isaiah 29:13** – "The Lord said, "Because this people draws near with their mouth and with their lips to honor me, but they have removed their heart far from me, and their fear of me is a commandment of men which has been taught."

**Isaiah 35:5-6** – "Then the eyes of the blind will be opened, and the ears of the deaf will be unstopped. Then the lame man will leap like a deer, and the tongue of the mute will sing; for waters will break out in the wilderness, and streams in the desert."

# WHY THESE PROPHECIES ARE IMPORTANT

In the references for chapter 15, we see the Fulfillment of the prophecy from Isaiah 35:5. We also saw this prophecy back in chapter 11. Again Jesus is healing people and casting out demons. This is a primary task the ancient prophecies said the Messiah would perform. Since Jesus is healing people, opening the eyes of the blind, and the ears of the deaf, we can know Jesus has the ability to heal people as was said of the prophesied Messiah.

Isaiah 29 is a new prophecy for us. This prophecy is in reference to all of the devout religious leaders who interact with Jesus. They speak the scriptures, but they do so in a condemning way, and do not convey the love of God. So the prophecy in Isaiah 29 tells us people give lip service to serving God, but they also teach people to be afraid of God. Thankfully, Isaiah 29 specifically tells us the fear of God is taught by men. Jesus tells us to love God with all of our heart, mind, and soul. God is a gracious, loving father who forgives us of our wrongdoings when we repent and ask for His forgiveness.

## WHAT STANDS OUT IN THESE PROPHECIES TO YOU?

## WHAT DO YOU THINK?

➢ Where do you see hypocrisy in Believers? What kind(s) of hypocrisies do you battle against, if any?

➢ What kinds of religious rules have people made by which they condemn themselves or others?

➤ Rather than being offended when we hear the truth about our sins, what would be a wiser way for us to respond?

_____

_____

_____

_____

_____

_____

_____

_____

➤ Based on the Canaanite woman's response to Jesus, how might you be able to pray more fervently when you are pleading a cause to God in your prayers?

_____

_____

_____

_____

_____

_____

_____

_____

➤ As part of the multitude who is learning about Jesus, what do you still wonder about Jesus? What kind(s) of questions do you have about Him?

_____

_____

_____

_____

_____

_____

_____

_____

- Jesus has compassion on the multitude and performs another miracle of feeding thousands from a few fish and seven loaves of bread. After witnessing the miracle of feeding 5000 a short time ago, why do you think the disciples asked Jesus where to get food to feed the multitude? Why are we so quick to forget the blessings we have received from God in the past?

___

# ACTION ITEM:

Three concepts taught in this chapter are 1) obedience to the intent of God's commands, 2) having strong faith in the Lord, and 3) having compassion on people. Of these three, with which do you struggle the most? Whether it is obedience, faith, or having compassion, what are some things you can do to begin overcoming your struggle:

___

# WHAT'S NEXT?

In the next chapter, we are presented with three more experiences with Jesus. In the first experience, Jesus discusses the signs of the times with the Pharisees and Sadducees. This first experience leads to the second, where Jesus' disciples misunderstand what Jesus says about yeast in bread. Lastly, Jesus asks His disciples who they say He is. As you read the next chapter, think about the signs of the times, how things rise and grow in your mind, and who you would say Jesus is.

# MATTHEW 16

The Pharisees and Sadducees came, and testing him, asked him to show them a sign from heaven. But he answered them, *"When it is evening, you say, 'It will be fair weather, for the sky is red.' In the morning, 'It will be foul weather today, for the sky is red and threatening.' Hypocrites! You know how to discern the appearance of the sky, but you can't discern the signs of the times! An evil and adulterous generation seeks after a sign, and there will be no sign given to it, except the sign of the prophet Jonah."*

He left them, and departed. The disciples came to the other side and had forgotten to take bread. Jesus said to them, *"Take heed and beware of the yeast of the Pharisees and Sadducees."*

They reasoned among themselves, saying, "We brought no bread."

Jesus, perceiving it, said, *"Why do you reason among yourselves, you of little faith, 'because you have brought no bread?' Don't you yet perceive, neither remember the five loaves for the five thousand, and how many baskets you took up? Nor the seven loaves for the four thousand, and how many baskets you took up? How is it that you don't perceive that I didn't speak to you concerning bread?*

*But beware of the yeast of the Pharisees and Sadducees."*

Then they understood that he didn't tell them to beware of the yeast of bread, but of the teaching of the Pharisees and Sadducees.

Now when Jesus came into the parts of Caesarea Philippi, he asked his disciples, saying, *"Who do men say that I, the Son of Man, am?"*

They said, "Some say John the Baptizer, some, Elijah, and others, Jeremiah, or one of the prophets."

He said to them, *"But who do you say that I am?"*

Simon Peter answered, "You are the Christ, the Son of the living God."

Jesus answered him, *"Blessed are you, Simon Bar Jonah, for flesh and blood has not revealed this to you, but my Father who is in heaven. I also tell you that you are Peter, and on this rock I will build my assembly, and the gates of Hades will not prevail against it. I will give to you the keys of the Kingdom of Heaven, and whatever you bind on earth will have been bound in heaven; and whatever you release on earth will have been released in heaven."*

Then he commanded the disciples that they should tell no one that he was Jesus the Christ. From that time, Jesus began to show his disciples that he must go to Jerusalem and suffer many things from the elders, chief priests, and scribes, and be killed, and the third day be raised up.

Peter took him aside, and began to rebuke him, saying, "Far be it from you, Lord! This will never be done to you."

But he turned, and said to Peter, *"Get behind me, Satan! You are a stumbling block to me, for you are not setting your mind on the things of God, but on the things of men."*

Then Jesus said to his disciples, *"If anyone desires to come after me, let him deny himself, and take up his cross, and follow me. For whoever desires to save his life will lose it, and whoever will lose his life for my sake will find it. For what will it profit a man, if he gains the whole world, and forfeits his life? Or what will a man give in exchange for his life?*

*"For the Son of Man will come in the glory of his Father with his angels, and then he will render to everyone according to his deeds. Most certainly I tell you, there are some standing here who will in no way taste of death, until they see the Son of Man coming in his Kingdom."*

## PROPHECIES IN THIS CHAPTER

**Jonah 1:17** – "The Lord prepared a great fish to swallow up Jonah, and Jonah was in the belly of the fish three days and three nights."

**Matthew 16:4** – "An evil and adulterous generation seeks after a sign, and there will be no sign given to it, except the sign of the prophet Jonah." (Here, we learn the sign of Jonah is a prophecy sign.)

**Matthew 16:21** – "Jesus began to show his disciples that he must go to Jerusalem and suffer many things from the elders, chief priests, and scribes, and be killed, and the third day be raised up." (Jesus prophecies his own suffering, death, and resurrection.)

**Malachi 4:5-6** – To read this prophecy again, see Prophecies in Chapter 11 of this book.

**Daniel 7:13-14** – To read this prophecy again, see Chapter 9 & 12 in this book.

**Isaiah 53:4-5** – To read this prophecy again, see Prophecies in Chapter 8 of this book.

**Isaiah 53:5-12** – But he was pierced for our transgressions. He was crushed for our iniquities. The punishment that brought our peace was on him; and by his wounds we are healed.

All we like sheep have gone astray. Everyone has turned to his own way; and The Lord has laid on him the iniquity of us all.

He was oppressed, yet when he was afflicted he didn't open his mouth. As a lamb that is led to the slaughter, and as a sheep that before its shearers is silent, so he didn't open his mouth.

He was taken away by oppression and judgment; and as for his generation, who considered that he was cut off out of the land of the living and stricken for the disobedience of my people?

They made his grave with the wicked, and with a rich man in his death; although he had done no violence, nor was any deceit in his mouth.

Yet it pleased The Lord to bruise him. He has caused him to suffer. When you make his soul an offering for sin, he will see his offspring. He will prolong his days, and The Lord's pleasure will prosper in his hand.

After the suffering of his soul, he will see the light and be satisfied. My righteous servant will justify many by the knowledge of himself; and he will bear their iniquities.

Therefore will I give him a portion with the great, and he will divide the plunder with the strong; because he poured out his soul to death, and was numbered with the transgressors; yet he bore the sin of many, and made intercession for the transgressors.

**Isaiah 22:22** – I will lay the key of David's house on his shoulder. He will open, and no one will shut. He will shut, and no one will open.

# WHY THESE PROPHECIES ARE IMPORTANT

Here in Matthew 16, we see a lot of references to prophecies we have already studied. I'll refer you back to the chapters where we covered those prophecies before, rather than present them again here.

In Matthew 16, Jesus makes a direct reference to the sign of Jonah. We talked about this prophecy in chapter 12. There the reference is a bit more obscure, but nevertheless it is a prophetic sign.

You can refer back to chapter 11 for an explanation of the Malachi 4 prophesy, if you want to refresh your memory. Refer back to chapters 9 & 12 for explanations of the Daniel 7 prophecy.

In this chapter, Jesus prophecies his own suffering, death, and resurrection. We already know these prophesies have happened. It is important to note: Jesus Himself was able to tell what would happen in the future, and we know that is a special gift (ability) of God.

Jesus speaks a prophecy by telling His disciples precisely what is going to happen to Him in Jerusalem in the near future. These events, which Jesus prophesized, were the fulfillment of the prophecy foretold thousands of years earlier in Isaiah 53.

I've cited some of the most applicable verses from Isaiah 53 in this prophecy listing for you. Jesus's persecution was prophesied in both Isaiah 53 and by Jesus himself in this chapter of Matthew. Because these prophecies came true, we know they came from God.

Also in this chapter, we see another reference to The House of David, as it relates to giving the Kingdom to the Messiah. We had a much deeper discussion about this prophecy in Matthew, Chapter 1.

# WHAT STANDS OUT IN THESE PROPHECIES TO YOU?

_____
_____
_____
_____
_____
_____
_____
_____
_____
_____
_____
_____
_____
_____
_____
_____
_____
_____

# WHAT DO YOU THINK?

- Why were the religious leaders seeking additional signs, when Jesus had already fulfilled many prophecies and performed many miracles? Why do people still fail to recognize the signs plainly spoken about in the Bible?

- Why does Jesus warn us to beware of the teaching of self-righteous religious leaders? What can you do to ensure you don't succumb to false teachings?

- Who would you say Jesus is to you? Why is He important to you?

- Jesus Christ is the living son of the Living God, on which God's assembly is being built. How does building God's assembly based on Jesus ensure the Gates of Hell will not prevail?

➤ In what ways are we stumbling blocks to Jesus when we don't have our minds on the things of God?

___

➤ What is the difference between losing your life for the sake of Jesus and finding it there, versus gaining the whole world only to find you actually forfeited your life? Where is everlasting life actually found?

___

## ACTION ITEM:

Think of one thing you can do to follow Jesus more closely, especially in the current times. Make a commitment to do this one thing!

## WHAT'S NEXT?

Perhaps you're beginning to notice a pattern in these chapters of Matthew's book. How many incidents with Jesus do you think are presented in the next chapter? There are THREE again!

In the next chapter, Jesus takes on a different bodily form, causing His disciples to fall on their faces. Then Jesus' disciples are unable to heal a boy with a demon, and one of the most certain things in life happens.. Jesus must pay taxes.

As you read the next chapter, think about what would your reaction be when Jesus changes bodily form. Also seek to understand why the disciples couldn't heal the boy who was possessed with a demon. The taxes are the same then as today.. we have to pay them, whether we have a miracle by which we can pay or not!

# MATTHEW 17

After six days, Jesus took with him Peter, James, and John his brother, and brought them up into a high mountain by themselves. He was changed before them. His face shone like the sun, and his garments became as white as the light. Behold, Moses and Elijah appeared to them talking with him.

Peter answered, and said to Jesus, "Lord, it is good for us to be here. If you want, let's make three tents here: one for you, one for Moses, and one for Elijah."

While he was still speaking, behold, a bright cloud overshadowed them. Behold, a voice came out of the cloud, saying, *"This is my beloved Son, in whom I am well pleased. Listen to him."*

When the disciples heard it, they fell on their faces, and were very afraid. Jesus came and touched them and said, *"Get up, and don't be afraid."* Lifting up their eyes, they saw no one, except Jesus alone. As they were coming down from the mountain, Jesus commanded them, saying, *"Don't tell anyone what you saw, until the Son of Man has risen from the dead."*

His disciples asked him, saying, "Then why do the scribes say that Elijah must come first?"

Jesus answered them, *"Elijah indeed comes first, and will restore all things, but I tell you that Elijah has come already, and they didn't recognize him, but did to him whatever they wanted to. Even so the Son of Man will also suffer by them."* Then the disciples understood that he spoke to them of John the Baptizer.

When they came to the multitude, a man came to him, kneeling down to him, and saying, "Lord, have mercy on my son, for he is epileptic, and suffers grievously; for he often falls into the fire, and often into the water. So I brought him to your disciples, and they could not cure him."

Jesus answered, *"Faithless and perverse generation! How long will I be with you? How long will I bear with you? Bring him here to me."* Jesus rebuked him, the demon went out of him, and the boy was cured from that hour.

Then the disciples came to Jesus privately, and said, "Why weren't we able to cast it out?"

He said to them, *"Because of your unbelief. For most certainly I tell you, if you have faith as a grain of mustard seed, you will tell this mountain, 'Move from here to there,' and it will move; and nothing will be impossible for you. But this kind doesn't go out except by prayer and fasting."*

While they were staying in Galilee, Jesus said to them, *"The Son of Man is about to be delivered up into the hands of men, and they will kill him, and the third day he will be raised up."*

They were exceedingly sorry.

When they had come to Capernaum, those who collected the didrachma coins came to Peter, and said, "Doesn't your teacher pay the didrachma?" He said, "Yes."

When he came into the house, Jesus anticipated him, saying, *"What do you think, Simon? From whom do the kings of the earth receive toll or tribute? From their children, or from strangers?"*

Peter said to him, "From strangers."

Jesus said to him, *"Therefore the children are exempt. But, lest we cause them to stumble, go to the sea, cast a hook, and take up the first fish that comes up. When you have opened its mouth, you will find a stater coin. Take that, and give it to them for me and you."*

## PROPHECIES IN THIS CHAPTER

**Malachi 4:5-6** – To read this prophecy again, see Prophecies in Chapter 11 of this book.

**Matthew 17:22-23** – "While they were staying in Galilee, Jesus said to them, 'The Son of Man is about to be delivered up into the hands of men, and they will kill him, and the third day he will be raised up.'" (This is the second time Jesus prophecies His own death)

**Daniel 7:9** - I saw until thrones were placed, and one who was ancient of days sat: his clothing was white as snow, and the hair of his head like pure wool; his throne was fiery flames, and its wheels burning fire.

**Daniel 8:18** - Now as he was speaking with me, I fell into a deep sleep with my face toward the ground; but he touched me, and set me upright.

**Daniel 10:18** - Then there touched me again one like the appearance of a man, and he strengthened me.

**Psalm 104:2** - He covers himself with light as with a garment. He stretches out the heavens like a curtain.

**Ezekiel 1:28** - As the appearance of the rainbow that is in the cloud in the day of rain, so was the appearance of the brightness all around. This was the appearance of the likeness of The Lord's glory. When I saw it, I fell on my face, and I heard a voice of one that spoke

**Exodus 3:6** - Moreover he said, "I am the God of your father, the God of Abraham, the God of Isaac, and the God of Jacob."

## WHY THESE PROPHECIES ARE IMPORTANT

For the second time, Jesus tells his followers about his upcoming crucifixion, death, and Resurrection. This prophecy of Jesus' is similar to the one in Matthew 16:21 in the previous chapter.

The Transfiguration of Jesus in this chapter, with his radiance and touching the disciples to lift them up, matches prophetic visions from the prophet, Daniel, and Psalm 104. The descriptors of Jesus include being "white as snow," "white as the light," and "he covers himself with light." These prophecies describe what the disciples saw on the top of the mountain when Jesus changed in appearance.

In both Daniel's vision and the disciple's experience, they became weak in the presence of Jesus' radiance. In both cases, Jesus stretches out his hand and touches them. His touch strengthens those in the presence of Jesus and helps them get up. When He did this, in both cases, He appeared again as a man.

The transfiguration is a most unusual event. The prophecies describe something that had never before happened. I'm sure the disciples, and no one else, ever expected Jesus to change his appearance and become radiant as light and white as snow. This is clearly a supernatural event, which only occurred with Jesus. The supporting prophecies are important because they provide a historical basis for the prediction of this otherwise unimaginable event.

# WHAT STANDS OUT IN THESE PROPHECIES TO YOU?

# WHAT DO YOU THINK?

➢ Moses and Elijah, long departed from Earth, appeared alive, were seen by men, and were talking with Christ at Jesus's transfiguration. What thoughts and questions would you have for Jesus, if you experienced seeing Moses and Elijah along with seeing Jesus transformed?

➢ God commands us to listen to Jesus! Why is this a critical command for everyone?

➢ Imagine you were present when Jesus was transformed. How would you refrain from telling anyone about Elijah, Moses, and Jesus, as Jesus requested? What would tempt you to tell someone?

➢ In what ways were the disciples faithless and perverse with their inability to heal the demon-possessed boy? Why do you think Jesus was "bearing with" the disciples at this point, given all they had already seen and experienced?

➢ What degree of faith do you have that nothing is impossible for you to do? What makes you hesitate to believe you can do anything, and what gives you confidence in your abilities?

➤ For the second time Jesus prophesied his own death and Resurrection. Why was this prophecy difficult for everyone to believe?

_____
_____
_____
_____
_____
_____
_____

## ACTION ITEM:

Reread the first paragraph of this chapter, as well as the prophecies from Daniel 7:9, Psalm 104:2, and Ezekiel 1:28. Notice the details of what Jesus looks like in the spirit. Then sit back, close your eyes, and see if you can picture in your mind the spiritual radiance and beauty of Christ's full glory, as described in the Bible.

## WHAT'S NEXT?

Jesus begins teaching again in the next chapter. Take note of where each teaching concept begins and ends. See if you can summarize each teaching in the journal space provided by condensing the teaching into one sentence. Contemplate which of Jesus' teaching(s) are most applicable to you and your life.

# MATTHEW 18

In that hour the disciples came to Jesus, saying, *"Who then is greatest in the Kingdom of Heaven?"*

Jesus called a little child to himself, and set him in the middle of them, and said, "*Most certainly I tell you, unless you turn, and become as little children, you will in no way enter into the Kingdom of Heaven.*

*"Whoever therefore humbles himself as this little child is the greatest in the Kingdom of Heaven. Whoever receives one such little child in my name receives me, but whoever causes one of these little ones who believe in me to stumble, it would be better for him if a huge millstone were hung around his neck, and that he were sunk in the depths of the sea.*

*"Woe to the world because of occasions of stumbling! For it must be that the occasions come, but woe to that person through whom the occasion comes! If your hand or your foot causes you to stumble, cut it off, and cast it from you. It is better for you to enter into life maimed or crippled, rather than having two hands or two feet to be cast into the eternal fire. If your eye causes you to stumble, pluck it out, and cast it from you. It is better for you to enter into life with one eye, rather than having two eyes to be cast into the Gehenna of fire.*

"See that you don't despise one of these little ones, for I tell you that in heaven their angels always see the face of my Father who is in heaven. For the Son of Man came to save that which was lost.

"What do you think? If a man has one hundred sheep, and one of them goes astray, doesn't he leave the ninety-nine, go to the mountains, and seek that which has gone astray? If he finds it, most certainly I tell you, he rejoices over it more than over the ninety-nine which have not gone astray. Even so it is not the will of your Father who is in heaven that one of these little ones should perish.

"If your brother sins against you, go, show him his fault between you and him alone. If he listens to you, you have gained back your brother. But if he doesn't listen, take one or two more with you, that at the mouth of two or three witnesses every word may be established. If he refuses to listen to them, tell it to the assembly. If he refuses to hear the assembly also, let him be to you as a Gentile or a tax collector.

"Most certainly I tell you, whatever things you bind on earth will have been bound in heaven, and whatever things you release on earth will have been released in heaven.

"Again, assuredly I tell you, that if two of you will agree on earth concerning anything that they will ask, it will be done for them by my Father who is in heaven. For where two or three are gathered together in my name, there I am in the middle of them."

Then Peter came and said to him, "Lord, how often shall my brother sin against me, and I forgive him? Until seven times?"

Jesus said to him, "*I don't tell you until seven times, but, until seventy times seven. Therefore the Kingdom of Heaven is like a certain king, who wanted to reconcile accounts with his servants. When he had begun to reconcile, one was brought to him who owed him ten thousand talents. But because he couldn't pay, his lord commanded him to be sold, with his wife, his children, and all that he had, and payment to be made. The servant therefore fell down and knelt before him, saying, 'Lord, have patience with me, and I will repay you all!'*

"The lord of that servant, being moved with compassion, released him, and forgave him the debt.

"But that servant went out, and found one of his fellow servants, who owed him one hundred denarii, and he grabbed him, and took him by the throat saying, 'Pay me what you owe!'

"So his fellow servant fell down at his feet and begged him, saying, 'Have patience with me, and I will repay you!'

"He would not, but went and cast him into prison, until he should pay back that which was due. So when his fellow servants saw what was done, they were exceedingly sorry, and came and told their lord all that was done. Then his lord called him in, and said to him, 'You wicked servant! I forgave you all that debt, because you begged me. Shouldn't you also have had mercy on your fellow servant, even as I had mercy on you?' His lord was angry, and delivered him to the tormentors, until he should pay all that was due to him. So my heavenly Father will also do to you, if you don't each forgive your brother from your hearts for his misdeeds."

## PROPHECIES IN THIS CHAPTER

NONE.

## WHAT DO YOU THINK?

➤ What characteristics of little children do you think we need in order to be able to enter Heaven?

➤ What causes you to stumble when you are trying to follow Jesus? What kinds of things do you do, which may cause others to stumble?

➢ God does not want anyone to perish. Who do you know that God needs to save? Write a short prayer for them, and begin to pray daily for God to save them.

_____
_____
_____
_____
_____
_____
_____

➢ Why do you think God wants us to go directly to a person who has sinned against us, rather than going to others first? If you hurt someone, how would you want them to handle your sin?

_____
_____
_____
_____
_____
_____
_____

➢ Who do you know that might need someone to pray with them, so two of you can be in agreement with your prayers? Who is someone that might be willing to pray regularly with you?

_____
_____
_____
_____
_____
_____
_____

> Who has done something for which you need to forgive them? What does Jesus say will happen if you don't forgive them?

## ACTION ITEM:

Make plans to pray with someone as two together. You can get together for coffee, a meal, meet online through video chat, or get together to pray in any way that works for you both. Consider finding someone you're willing to ask to become your regular prayer partner.

## WHAT'S NEXT?

In the next chapter, people have questions for Jesus. He answers questions about divorce, how to have eternal life, and Peter asks about the disciples' rewards for following Jesus. Think about questions you might have for Jesus. Make a note of questions you would like to have answered:

# MATTHEW 19

When Jesus had finished these words, he departed from Galilee, and came into the borders of Judea beyond the Jordan. Great multitudes followed him, and he healed them there. Pharisees came to him, testing him, and saying, "Is it lawful for a man to divorce his wife for any reason?"

He answered, *"Haven't you read that he who made them from the beginning made them male and female, and said, 'For this cause a man shall leave his father and mother, and shall be joined to his wife; and the two shall become one flesh?' So that they are no more two, but one flesh. What therefore God has joined together, don't let man tear apart."*

They asked him, "Why then did Moses command us to give her a certificate of divorce, and divorce her?"

He said to them, *"Moses, because of the hardness of your hearts, allowed you to divorce your wives, but from the beginning it has not been so. I tell you that whoever divorces his wife, except for sexual immorality, and marries another, commits adultery; and he who marries her when she is divorced commits adultery."*

His disciples said to him, "If this is the case of

the man with his wife, it is not expedient to marry."

But he said to them, *"Not all men can receive this saying, but those to whom it is given. For there are eunuchs who were born that way from their mother's womb, and there are eunuchs who were made eunuchs by men; and there are eunuchs who made themselves eunuchs for the Kingdom of Heaven's sake. He who is able to receive it, let him receive it."*

Then little children were brought to him, that he should lay his hands on them and pray; and the disciples rebuked them. But Jesus said, *"Allow the little children, and don't forbid them to come to me; for the Kingdom of Heaven belongs to ones like these."* He laid his hands on them, and departed from there.

Behold, one came to him and said, "Good teacher, what good thing shall I do, that I may have eternal life?"

He said to him, *"Why do you call me good? No one is good but one, that is, God. But if you want to enter into life, keep the commandments."*

He said to him, "Which ones?"

Jesus said, *"'You shall not murder.' 'You shall not commit adultery.' 'You shall not steal.' 'You shall not offer false testimony.' 'Honor your father and your mother.' And, 'You shall love your neighbor as yourself.'"*

The young man said to him, "All these things I have observed from my youth. What do I still lack?"

Jesus said to him, *"If you want to be perfect, go, sell what you have, and give to the poor, and you will have treasure in heaven; and come, follow me."* But when the young man heard the saying, he went away sad, for he was one who had great possessions.

Jesus said to his disciples, *"Most certainly I say to you, a rich man will enter into the Kingdom of Heaven with difficulty. Again I tell you, it is easier for a camel to go through a needle's eye, than for a rich man to enter into God's Kingdom."*

When the disciples heard it, they were exceedingly astonished, saying, "Who then can be saved?"

Looking at them, Jesus said, *"With men this is impossible, but with God all things are possible."*

Then Peter answered, "Behold, we have left everything, and followed you. What then will we have?"

Jesus said to them, *"Most certainly I tell you that you who have followed me, in the regeneration when the Son of Man will sit on the throne of his glory, you also will sit on twelve thrones, judging the twelve tribes of Israel. Everyone who has left houses, or brothers, or sisters, or father, or mother, or wife, or children, or lands, for my name's sake, will receive one hundred times, and will inherit eternal life. But many will be last who are first; and first who are last.*

# PROPHECIES IN THIS CHAPTER
NONE.

# WHAT DO YOU THINK?

➢ What is the only valid reason to seek a divorce in God's eyes? Why?

➢ God forgives us no matter what our sins are, except for blasphemy, as we learned in Matthew 12. Thus, people who have gotten divorced are forgiven, yet God hates divorce. What are some things people can do instead of getting divorced, if they are in a stressful marriage?

➢ List the six Commandments Jesus says we must follow. Circle or highlight the Commandments which are difficult for you to keep. Ask God to help you learn to obey these Commandments.

___

➢ Why do you think it's difficult for rich people to get into heaven?

___

➢ Since all things are possible with God, and God can save anyone from anything, what do you most want God to help you change about yourself?

___

➢ What makes a person first or last on Earth? What do you think makes a person first or last in heaven?

_____
_____
_____
_____
_____
_____
_____

# ACTION ITEM:

What questions do you still have, which Jesus did not answer? Go to BibleHub.com or BibleGateway.com (or both), then type the topic of your question. See what you can discover about these topics from a Biblical point of view.

# WHAT'S NEXT?

In the next chapter, we again encounter three incidents with Jesus. First, we learn more about what the Kingdom of Heaven is like. The second incident is an unusual request made by the mom of two of Jesus' disciples. And the third incident is a healing miracle which Jesus performs. Consider how you feel about each of these incidents. Analyze what makes you feel uncomfortable within each situation, and focus on why these are uncomfortable situations for many people.

# MATTHEW 20

"For the Kingdom of Heaven is like a man who was the master of a household, who went out early in the morning to hire laborers for his vineyard. When he had agreed with the laborers for a denarius a day, he sent them into his vineyard. He went out about the third hour, and saw others standing idle in the marketplace. He said to them, 'You also go into the vineyard, and whatever is right I will give you.' So they went their way. Again he went out about the sixth and the ninth hour, and did likewise. About the eleventh hour he went out, and found others standing idle. He said to them, 'Why do you stand here all day idle?'

"They said to him, 'Because no one has hired us.'

"He said to them, 'You also go into the vineyard, and you will receive whatever is right.' When evening had come, the lord of the vineyard said to his manager, 'Call the laborers and pay them their wages, beginning from the last to the first.'

"When those who were hired at about the eleventh hour came, they each received a denarius. When the first came, they supposed that they would receive more; and they likewise each received a denarius. When they received it, they murmured against the master of the household, saying, 'These last have spent one hour, and you have made them equal to us, *who have borne the burden of the day and the scorching heat!'*

*"But he answered one of them, 'Friend, I am doing you no wrong. Didn't you agree with me for a denarius? Take that which is yours, and go your way. It is my desire to give to this last just as much as to you. Isn't it lawful for me to do what I want to with what I own? Or is your eye evil, because I am good?' So the last will be first, and the first last. For many are called, but few are chosen."*

As Jesus was going up to Jerusalem, he took the twelve disciples aside, and on the way he said to them, *"Behold, we are going up to Jerusalem, and the Son of Man will be delivered to the chief priests and scribes, and they will condemn him to death, and will hand him over to the Gentiles to mock, to scourge, and to crucify; and the third day he will be raised up."*

Then the mother of the sons of Zebedee came to him with her sons, kneeling and asking a certain thing of him. He said to her, *"What do you want?"*

She said to him, "Command that these, my two sons, may sit, one on your right hand, and one on your left hand, in your Kingdom."

But Jesus answered, *"You don't know what you are asking. Are you able to drink the cup that I am about to drink, and be baptized with the baptism that I am baptized with?"*

They said to him, "We are able."

He said to them, *"You will indeed drink my cup, and be baptized with the baptism that I am baptized with, but to sit on my right hand and on my left hand is not mine to give; but it is for whom it has been prepared by my Father."*

When the ten heard it, they were indignant with the two brothers.

But Jesus summoned them, and said, *"You know that the rulers of the nations lord it over them, and their great ones exercise authority over them. It shall not be so among you, but whoever desires to become great among you shall be your servant. Whoever desires to be first among you shall be your bondservant, even as the Son of Man came not to be served, but to serve, and to give his life as a ransom for many."*

As they went out from Jericho, a great multitude followed him. Behold, two blind men sitting by the road, when they heard that Jesus was passing by, cried out, "Lord, have mercy on us, you son of David!" The multitude rebuked them, telling them that they should be quiet, but they cried out even more, "Lord, have mercy on us, you son of David!"

Jesus stood still, and called them, and asked, *"What do you want me to do for you?"*

They told him, "Lord, that our eyes may be opened." Jesus, being moved with compassion, touched their eyes; and immediately their eyes received their sight, and they followed him.

# PROPHECIES IN THIS CHAPTER

**Daniel 9:25-27** – Know therefore and discern, that from the going out of the commandment to restore and to build Jerusalem to the Anointed One, the prince, shall be seven weeks, and sixty-two weeks: it shall be built again, with street and moat, even in troubled times. After the sixty-two weeks the Anointed One shall be cut off, and shall have nothing: and the people of the prince who shall come shall destroy the city and the sanctuary; and its end shall be with a flood, and even to the end shall be war; desolations are determined. He shall make a firm covenant with many for one week: and in the middle of the week he shall cause the sacrifice and the offering to cease; and on the wing of abominations shall come one who makes desolate; and even to the full end, and that determined, shall wrath be poured out on the desolate.

**Isaiah 53:5-12** – To reread and review this prophecy, see chapter 16.

**2 Samuel 7:12-16** – When your days are fulfilled, and you sleep with your fathers, I will set up your offspring after you, who will proceed out of your body, and I will establish his kingdom. He will build a house for my name, and I will establish the throne of his kingdom forever. I will be his father, and he will be my son. If he commits iniquity, I will chasten him with the rod of men, and with the stripes of the children of men; but my loving kindness will not depart from him, as I took it from Saul, whom I put away before you. Your house and your kingdom will be made sure forever before you. Your throne will be established forever.

**Isaiah 35:5-6** – To reread and review this prophecy, see chapter 15.

**Matthew 20:18-19** – "Behold, we are going up to Jerusalem, and the Son of Man will be delivered to the chief priests and scribes, and they will condemn him to death, and will hand him over to the Gentiles to mock, to scourge, and to crucify; and the third day he will be raised up."

# WHY THESE PROPHECIES ARE IMPORTANT

The first Prophecy from Daniel seems somewhat obscure. However, researching a variety of references, they consistently say this prophecy relates to the timing of the Messiah's appearance and the destruction of the temple in Jerusalem.

The prophecy indicates the Messiah will come, be cut off, then the temple will be destroyed in Jerusalem. These events can never occur again in history, because the temple is destroyed already. No one else can come before the temple is destroyed. Therefore, the candidates for Messiah can only come from our past history, up until the destruction of the temple in 70 AD.

When the temple was destroyed, it indicated with finality the Messiah had already come according to this ancient prophecy. So, if you believe in God and in his prophecies, your choices for Messiah must come from among men who lived before 70 AD, when the temple in Jerusalem was destroyed.

Timing-wise, and based on the evidence from the collection of ancient prophesies, Jesus is the only person who fits this prophecy and many of the prophecies we have already covered. No one can come after Him, since the temple has already been destroyed. Who, among those who lived before 70 A.D., would even come into consideration as the true Messiah besides Jesus?

Another important aspect of this prophecy from Daniel 9:27 is that the sacrifices and offerings will be caused to cease when the Messiah comes and the temple is destroyed. The Jewish people no longer conduct sacrifices and offerings on an altar. This is another independent fulfillment of an ancient prophecy regarding what will happen when the Messiah comes. And indeed—it has already happened, because the sacrifices and offerings ceased after the temple was destroyed.

In this chapter, we again see a prophetic reference to Isaiah 53. The first time we saw these verses was in chapter 16. You can read about the this prophecy in Chapter 16's prophecy section.

The prophecies from 2 Samuel 7 are from the prophet Nathan telling King David what God has told him regarding David's throne enduring forever. This is not a new prophecy concept to us. Instead, it is a reiteration of the promise David would have a son who would reign after him, and there will be an heir down the line from David who will remain on the throne forever. As we now know, the eternal reigning King is apparently Jesus Christ.

We also see the prophecy from Isaiah 35 again regarding the Messiah healing people. You can review what we said about Isaiah 35 in the prophecy notes from chapter 15. At this point, we know Jesus healed many people.

Lastly, for the third time, Jesus tells his followers about His upcoming crucifixion, death, and resurrection. This prophecy of Jesus' is similar to the ones in Matthew 16:21 and Matthew 17:22-23. As you will know by the end of the book of Matthew, this prophecy has already been fulfilled.

Many of these prophecies are presented again, because they are referenced in many versions of the Bible as foundational Concepts for this chapter in the Book of Matthew. While these are not all new prophecies, the number of prophecies pertaining to Jesus has grown significantly, thereby making it unlikely the Messiah is anyone other than Jesus.

# WHAT STANDS OUT IN THESE PROPHECIES TO YOU?

# WHAT DO YOU THINK?

- If it's lawful for God to do whatever He wants with everything He owns, is it proper for people to begrudge God when things don't go the way they want? Explain your thoughts and feelings.

- For the third and final time, Jesus tells His disciples He will be killed and will be raised up on the third day. What benefit exists in Jesus repeating this prophecy about His death and Resurrection?

➤ What kind(s) of sin(s) led James' and John's mother to ask for her sons to have the highest positions in Heaven?

_____
_____
_____
_____
_____
_____
_____

➤ Do you think you would or could withstand physical abuse and suffering to defend Christianity to the point of your own death? What would it take for a person to be able to defend Christianity while being tortured and killed for believing Jesus Christ is the Messiah?

_____
_____
_____
_____
_____
_____
_____
_____

➤ In your life right now, how much of your free time is spent serving others, being served, or neither? If you could serve anyone you want, doing anything worthwhile, what are some ways you would choose to serve others?

_____
_____
_____
_____
_____
_____
_____
_____

➤ Imagine Jesus asks you, "What do you want me to do for you?" What would be your request?

_____
_____
_____
_____
_____
_____
_____
_____
_____

# ACTION ITEM:

Write your own creative description of what you think the Kingdom of Heaven will be like:

_____
_____
_____
_____
_____
_____
_____
_____
_____
_____
_____
_____
_____

# WHAT'S NEXT?

What do a donkey, tables in the temple, a fig tree, and a stone have to do with Jesus? In the next chapter, some interesting events occur in Jesus' life during the week before His crucifixion. Pay the closest attention to how Jesus describes Himself in the context of a stone. Think about the ways people reject, trip over, and use stones, especially as stones relate to Jesus being our cornerstone.

# MATTHEW 21

When they came near to Jerusalem, and came to Bethsphage, to the Mount of Olives, then Jesus sent two disciples, saying to them, *"Go into the village that is opposite you, and immediately you will find a donkey tied, and a colt with her. Untie them, and bring them to me. If anyone says anything to you, you shall say, 'The Lord needs them,' and immediately he will send them."*

All this was done, that it might be fulfilled which was spoken through the prophet, saying,

"Tell the daughter of Zion, behold, your King comes to you, humble, and riding on a donkey, on a colt, the foal of a donkey."

The disciples went, and did just as Jesus commanded them, and brought the donkey and the colt, and laid their clothes on them; and he sat on them. A very great multitude spread their clothes on the road. Others cut branches from the trees, and spread them on the road. The multitudes who went in front of him, and those who followed, kept shouting, "Hosanna to the son of David! Blessed is he who comes in the name of the Lord! Hosanna in the highest!"

When he had come into Jerusalem, all the city was stirred up, saying, "Who is this?" The multitudes said, "This is the prophet, Jesus, from Nazareth of Galilee."

Jesus entered into the temple of God, and drove out all of those who sold and bought in the temple, and overthrew the money changers' tables and the seats of those who sold the doves. He said to them, *"It is written, 'My house shall be called a house of prayer,' but you have made it a den of robbers!"*

The blind and the lame came to him in the temple, and he healed them. But when the chief priests and the scribes saw the wonderful things that he did, and the children who were crying in the temple and saying, "Hosanna to the son of David!" they were indignant, and said to him, "Do you hear what these are saying?"

Jesus said to them, *"Yes. Did you never read, 'Out of the mouth of babes and nursing babies you have perfected praise?'"*

He left them, and went out of the city to Bethany, and camped there.

Now in the morning, as he returned to the city, he was hungry. Seeing a fig tree by the road, he came to it, and found nothing on it but leaves. He said to it, *"Let there be no fruit from you forever!"*

Immediately the fig tree withered away. When the disciples saw it, they marveled, saying, "How did the fig tree immediately wither away?"

Jesus answered them, *"Most certainly I tell you, if you have faith, and don't doubt, you will not only do what was done to the fig tree, but even if you told this mountain, 'Be taken up and cast into the sea,' it would be done. All things, whatever you ask in prayer, believing, you will receive."*

When he had come into the temple, the chief priests and the elders of the people came to him as he was teaching, and said, "By what authority do you do these things? Who gave you this authority?"

Jesus answered them, *"I also will ask you one question, which if you tell me, I likewise will tell you by what authority I do these things. The baptism of John, where was it from? From heaven or from men?"*

They reasoned with themselves, saying, "If we say, 'From heaven,' he will ask us, 'Why then did you not believe him?' But if we say, 'From men,' we fear the multitude, for all hold John as a prophet." They answered Jesus, and said, "We don't know."

He also said to them, *"Neither will I tell you by what authority I do these things. But what do you think?*

*"A man had two sons, and he came to the first, and said, 'Son, go work today in my vineyard.' He answered, 'I will not,' but afterward he changed his mind, and went.*

*"He came to the second, and said the same thing. He answered, 'I'm going, sir,' but he didn't go. Which of the two did the will of his father?"*

They said to him, "The first."

Jesus said to them, *"Most certainly I tell you that the tax collectors and the prostitutes are entering into God's Kingdom before you. For John came to you in the way of righteousness, and you didn't believe him, but the tax collectors and the prostitutes believed him. When you saw it, you didn't even repent afterward, that you might believe him.*

*"Hear another parable. There was a man who was a master of a household, who planted a vineyard, set a hedge about it, dug a wine press in it, built a tower, leased it out to farmers, and went into another country. When the season for the fruit came near, he sent his servants to the farmers, to receive his fruit. The farmers took his servants, beat one, killed another, and stoned another.*

*"Again, he sent other servants more than the first: and they treated them the same way. But afterward he sent to them his son, saying, 'They will respect my son.' But the farmers, when they saw the son, said among themselves, 'This is the heir. Come, let's kill him, and seize his inheritance.' So they took him, and threw him out of the vineyard, and killed him. When therefore the lord of the vineyard comes, what will he do to those farmers?"*

They told him, "He will miserably destroy those miserable men, and will lease out the vineyard to other farmers, who will give him the fruit in its season."

Jesus said to them, *"Did you never read in the Scriptures, 'The stone which the builders rejected was made the head of the corner. This was from the Lord. It is marvelous in our eyes?'*

*"Therefore I tell you, God's Kingdom will be taken away from you, and will be given to a nation producing its fruit. He who falls on this stone will be broken to pieces, but on whomever it will fall, it will scatter him as dust."*

When the chief priests and the Pharisees heard his parables, they perceived that he spoke about them. When they sought to seize him, they feared the multitudes, because they considered him to be a prophet.

## PROPHECIES IN THIS CHAPTER

**Matthew 21:1b-3** – "Then Jesus sent to disciples, saying to them, "Go into the village that is opposite you, and immediately you will find a donkey tied, and a colt with her. Untie them, and bring them to me. If anyone says anything to you, you shall say, 'The Lord needs them,' and immediately he will send them."

**Zechariah 9:9** – "Rejoice greatly, daughter of Zion! Shout, daughter of Jerusalem! Behold, your King comes to you! He is righteous, and having salvation; lowly, and riding on a donkey, even on a colt, the foal of a donkey."

**Psalm 69:9** – "For the zeal of your house consumes me. The reproaches of those who reproach you have fallen on me."

**Psalm 118:22-24** – "The stone which the builders rejected has become the head of the corner. This is The Lord's doing. It is marvelous in our eyes. This is the day that The Lord has made. We will rejoice and be glad in it!"

**Psalm 118:26-27** – "Blessed is he who comes in The Lord's name! We have blessed you out of The Lord's house. The Lord is God, and he has given us light. Bind the sacrifice with cords, even to the horns of the altar."

**Deuteronomy 18:15-19** – To reread and review this prophecy, see chapter 13.

**Isaiah 8:14-15** – He will be a sanctuary, but for both houses of Israel, he will be a trap and a snare for the inhabitants of Jerusalem. Many will stumble over it, fall, be broken, be snared, and be captured."

**Daniel 2:34-35** – You saw until a stone was cut out without hands, which struck the image on its feet that were of iron and clay, and broke them in pieces. Then was the iron, the clay, the brass, the silver, and the gold, broken in pieces together, and became like the chaff of the summer threshing floors; and the wind carried them away, so that no place was found for them: and the stone that struck the image became a great mountain, and filled the whole earth.

**Psalm 80:7-11** – Turn us again, God of Armies. Cause your face to shine, and we will be saved. You brought a vine out of Egypt. You drove out the nations, and planted it.

You cleared the ground for it. It took deep root, and filled the land.

The mountains were covered with its shadow. Its boughs were like God's cedars.

It sent out its branches to the sea, Its shoots to the River.

**Jeremiah 7:11** – Has this house, which is called by my name, become a den of robbers in your eyes? Behold, I, even I, have seen it," says The Lord.

**Isaiah 5:1-2** – Let me sing for my well beloved a song of my beloved about his vineyard. My beloved had a vineyard on a very fruitful hill. He dug it up, gathered out its stones, planted it with the choicest vine, built a tower in the middle of it, and also cut out a wine press therein. He looked for it to yield grapes, but it yielded wild grapes.

# WHY THESE PROPHECIES ARE IMPORTANT

One of the shortest spans of time between Jesus speaking a prophecy and its fulfillment is given in Matthew 21. Jesus told his disciples they would find a donkey when they went into the village. They found a donkey, just as Jesus said they would. Jesus also told them what to say if anyone asked questions. The disciples answered exactly as Jesus told them to answer.

In an unexpected prophecy from God, prophet Zechariah says, "Behold, your king comes to you lowly and riding on a donkey. He is righteous and has salvation." Who would expect a king would come riding into town on a donkey? This is a unique prophecy which was fulfilled when Jesus came into Jerusalem riding on the donkey He told His disciples they would find.

Again, this is one of those prophecies, like being born of a virgin, which people wouldn't make up if they were trying to convince a lot of people that Jesus is the King of all creation. These unexpected events are one reason the Jewish people do not believe that Jesus is truly their king. He does not fit their idea of who should be their king. However, Jesus fits God's prophetic description of their King.

Psalm 118 gives us the phrase people chanted as Jesus rode into town. They cried out, "Blessed is he who comes in the name of the Lord!" We also see in Psalm 118, Jesus is the stone which the builders rejected. This verse probably didn't make a lot of sense in the ancient days when it was written, because people thought it referred to the rejection of a literal stone in a physical temple that was going to be built. However the stone that is rejected figuratively represents Jesus, and He is rejected by the Jewish people, who are the original people in God's spiritual house.

Psalm 69 refers to Jesus' zeal for the temple of God. This prophecy describes the Messiah's passion for God's house. We see this prophecy in action when Jesus clears the money changers out of God's temple. In addition to the prophecy about this event, we have Jeremiah's reference to the Lord's House becoming a den of robbers.

The prophecy from Deuteronomy 18:15-19 was presented in Chapter 13. You can refer back to the prophecy notes there to refresh your memory about these verses in Deuteronomy.

The prophets Daniel and Isaiah also talk about Jesus as a stone which the builders rejected. We briefly mentioned this concept when we looked at the prophecy from Psalm 118. Here, it's important to realize the new temple for God's Holy Spirit is not a building created by human hands. The new temple is created when His Holy Spirit comes to live in our hearts. We become temples for God's Spirit.

His Holy Spirit comes into us when we acknowledge Jesus as God's Son and as our Savior. We are the temple for the Lord's spirit, so His Kingdom can stretch beyond any building a person may build.

Therefore, God's Kingdom fills the whole earth, just as it was prophesied.

Psalm 80 and the prophecy from Isaiah talk about God's kingdom as a Vineyard. Psalm 80 says God brought a vine out of Egypt. If you recall back in the early days of Jesus's life, He spent time in Egypt, out of which God called Him. God cleared the ground for Jesus as a Vineyard, and His vineyard grows and fills the land. Mountains are covered and it sends out branches to the seas and to the rivers. I love the verse at the end of the prophecy in Isaiah, which says He looked for His vineyard to yield grapes, but it yielded wild grapes! God is looking for fruit in our lives—good fruit. However, people on earth are wild of heart and do not faithfully produce good fruit for the benefit of God's Kingdom.

These verses about God's kingdom and his Sanctuary are important to us, because they explain how the Messiah's Kingdom was prophesied to grow and spread throughout the Earth. It has spread, and Jesus has followers throughout the world. His kingdom continued to spread after He was crucified, dead and buried, because He was resurrected. He's a Living spirit within the world and within our lives. He continues to grow people's hearts and minds toward faithfulness and righteousness in God.

# WHAT STANDS OUT IN THESE PROPHECIES TO YOU?

___

___

___

___

___

___

___

___

___

___

# WHAT DO YOU THINK?

➢ Zacharias' ancient prophecy said the Messiah would come humbly and riding on a donkey. What kind of kingship would you expect from a king who comes riding on a donkey? How might expectations be different for common people versus leaders and authorities in the country?

___

___

___

___

___

___

___

___

➤ In what ways are the words of small children more meaningful than the words of adults?

_____
_____
_____
_____
_____
_____
_____
_____
_____

➤ The fig tree didn't fulfill its God-given purpose of producing figs. What can we learn from Jesus's reaction to the fig tree?

_____
_____
_____
_____
_____
_____
_____
_____
_____

➤ What would help strengthen your faith, so you would no longer, or seldom, have doubts about God answering your prayers?

_____
_____
_____
_____
_____
_____
_____
_____
_____

➢ What characteristics of the chief priests and elders show they are working against God and His kingdom, rather than for it? What characteristics reveal whether a church leader is self-serving or is a true follower of Christ?

_____
_____
_____
_____
_____
_____
_____

➢ We are like farmers who are given an assignment to grow God's Kingdom. What skills do you need to cultivate in order to be more effective in helping God grow His Kingdom?

_____
_____
_____
_____
_____
_____
_____
_____
_____
_____

## ACTION ITEM:

Visit https://jewsforjesus.org/featured-articles/. Read articles which interest you, especially those pertaining to prophecies about Jesus. I especially like the article titled, "What Proof Do You Have That Jesus Was The Messiah?"

## WHAT'S NEXT?

In the next chapter, Jesus again describes what the Kingdom of Heaven is like using a parable as an illustration. Jesus is asked about taxes, marriage as it relates to Heaven, and what is the greatest commandment. Jesus asks the Pharisees a question, which they cannot answer. At this point in the study, consider what your answer would be, if you were giving an answer to the Pharisees.

# MATTHEW 22

Jesus answered and spoke to them again in parables, saying,

*"The Kingdom of Heaven is like a certain king, who made a wedding feast for his son, and sent out his servants to call those who were invited to the wedding feast, but they would not come. Again he sent out other servants, saying, 'Tell those who are invited, "Behold, I have prepared my dinner. My cattle and my fatlings are killed, and all things are ready. Come to the wedding feast!" ' But they made light of it, and went their ways, one to his own farm, another to his merchandise, and the rest grabbed his servants, and treated them shamefully, and killed them. When the king heard that, he was angry, and sent his armies, destroyed those murderers, and burned their city.*

*"Then he said to his servants, 'The wedding is ready, but those who were invited weren't worthy. Go therefore to the intersections of the highways, and as many as you may find, invite to the wedding feast.' Those servants went out into the highways, and gathered together as many as they found, both bad and good. The wedding was filled with guests. But when the king came in to see the guests, he saw there a man who didn't have on wedding clothing, and he said to him, 'Friend, how did you come in here not*

*wearing wedding clothing?' He was speechless. Then the king said to the servants, 'Bind him hand and foot, take him away, and throw him into the outer darkness. That is where the weeping and grinding of teeth will be.' For many are called, but few chosen."*

Then the Pharisees went and took counsel how they might entrap him in his talk. They sent their disciples to him, along with the Herodians, saying, "Teacher, we know that you are honest, and teach the way of God in truth, no matter whom you teach, for you aren't partial to anyone. Tell us therefore, what do you think? Is it lawful to pay taxes to Caesar, or not?"

But Jesus perceived their wickedness, and said, *"Why do you test me, you hypocrites? Show me the tax money."*

They brought to him a denarius.

He asked them, *"Whose is this image and inscription?"*

They said to him, "Caesar's."

Then he said to them, *"Give therefore to Caesar the things that are Caesar's, and to God the things that are God's."*

When they heard it, they marveled, and left him, and went away.

On that day Sadducees (those who say that there is no resurrection) came to him. They asked him, saying, "Teacher, Moses said, 'If a man dies, having no children, his brother shall marry his wife, and raise up offspring for his brother.' Now there were with us seven brothers. The first married and died, and having no offspring left his wife to his brother. In the same way, the second also, and the third, to the seventh. After them all, the woman died. In the resurrection therefore, whose wife will she be of the seven? For they all had her."

But Jesus answered them, *"You are mistaken, not knowing the Scriptures, nor the power of God. For in the resurrection they neither marry, nor are given in marriage, but are like God's angels in heaven. But concerning the resurrection of the dead, haven't you read that which was spoken to you by God, saying,*

*'I am the God of Abraham, and the God of Isaac, and the God of Jacob?' God is not the God of the dead, but of the living."*

When the multitudes heard it, they were astonished at his teaching. But the Pharisees, when they heard that he had silenced the Sadducees, gathered themselves together. One of them, a lawyer, asked him a question, testing him.

"Teacher, which is the greatest commandment in the law?"

Jesus said to him, " *'You shall love the Lord your God with all your heart, with all your soul, and with all your mind.' This is the first and great commandment. A second likewise is this, 'You shall love your neighbor as yourself.' The whole law and the prophets depend on these two commandments."*

Now while the Pharisees were gathered together, Jesus asked them a question, saying, *"What do you think of the Christ? Whose son is he?"*

They said to him, "Of David."

He said to them, *"How then does David in the Spirit call him Lord, saying, 'The Lord said to my Lord, sit on my right hand, until I make your enemies a footstool for your feet?*

*"If then David calls him Lord, how is he his son?"*

No one was able to answer him a word, neither did any man dare ask him any more questions from that day forward.

# PROPHECIES IN THIS CHAPTER

**Psalm 110:1-4** – "The Lord says to my Lord, 'Sit at my right hand, until I make your enemies your footstool for your feet.' The Lord will send out the rod of your strength out of Zion. Rule among your enemies. Your people offer themselves willingly in the day of your power, in holy array. Out of the womb of the morning, you have the dew of your youth. The Lord has sworn, and will not change his mind: 'You are a priest forever in the order of Melchizedek.'"

# WHY THIS PROPHECY IS IMPORTANT

Here in chapter 22 of Matthew, Jesus refers to Psalm 110 in which David says, "The Lord said to my Lord, sit on my right hand." This is an interesting prophecy, because it is one of the earliest introductions to the concept of the Father and the Son as two distinct persons, yet part of one godhead. The two lords, where the Lord said to my Lord, carry different meanings in the original language. The first Lord is God the Father Almighty, the Lord. The second Lord is Jesus, our Lord, the Son, who is part of the Trinity of the Father, Son, and Holy Spirit. Each of these entities is God, all-in-one, yet distinct also. So an easier reading of this would be, "God said to Jesus, sit on my right hand, until I make your enemies a footstool for your feet."

## WHAT STANDS OUT IN THIS PROPHECY TO YOU?

## WHAT DO YOU THINK?

➢ Many people are invited to share in Jesus's Kingdom, but they reject His invitation. If you accepted Jesus's invitation to join Him, what made you accept His invitation? If not yet, what holds you back?

➢ The man without wedding clothes is representative of people who haven't put on the spiritual righteousness of Christ. Even though they believe in God. They're living for themselves, doing what they want, and aren't following Jesus. What evidence is visible when a person is truly following Jesus Christ?

➤ We must pay our taxes to the government, but give God our hearts and souls. How can you give yourself to Jesus? What does it look like to give your heart and soul to Him?

_____

_____

_____

_____

_____

_____

_____

_____

➤ The Sadducees were mistaken about the Kingdom of Heaven, because they did not know scriptures. Why is it important for you to learn all you can about God and His Word in the Bible?

_____

_____

_____

_____

_____

_____

_____

_____

➤ Do you truly obey the greatest commandment, to love the Lord your God with all your heart, soul, and mind? What do you need to change or do in order to give God your heartfelt spiritual love?

_____

_____

_____

_____

_____

_____

_____

_____

➤ If the whole law is fulfilled when you love God with all your heart, soul, and mind, and when you love other people like yourself, what prevents you from fulfilling the whole law in this way?

_____
_____
_____
_____
_____
_____

# ACTION ITEM:

Make a list of things you have which belong to God versus the government.

| **Belongs to God:** | **Belongs to the Government:** |
|---|---|
|  |  |
|  |  |
|  |  |
|  |  |
|  |  |
|  |  |
|  |  |
|  |  |
|  |  |
|  |  |
|  |  |
|  |  |
|  |  |

# WHAT'S NEXT?

The entirety of the next chapter is Jesus speaking to the multitudes. He issues a series of "woe to you" statements, which focus on the wrongdoings of certain people. Pay close attention to the behaviors Jesus points out as bringing woe upon those people. Seek to discover areas where you might need to make changes in your way of living or interacting with other people. Circle or highlight those behaviors which are a problem in your life.

# MATTHEW 23

Then Jesus spoke to the multitudes and to his disciples, saying, "*The scribes and the Pharisees sat on Moses' seat. All things therefore whatever they tell you to observe, observe and do, but don't do their works; for they say, and don't do. For they bind heavy burdens that are grievous to be borne, and lay them on men's shoulders; but they themselves will not lift a finger to help them. But they do all their works to be seen by men. They make their phylacteries broad, enlarge the fringes of their garments, and love the place of honor at feasts, the best seats in the synagogues, the salutations in the marketplaces, and to be called 'Rabbi, Rabbi' by men. But don't you be called 'Rabbi,' for one is your teacher, the Christ, and all of you are brothers. Call no man on the earth your father, for one is your Father, he who is in heaven. Neither be called masters, for one is your master, the Christ. But he who is greatest among you will be your servant. Whoever exalts himself will be humbled, and whoever humbles himself will be exalted.*

*"Woe to you, scribes and Pharisees, hypocrites!*
*"For you devour widows' houses, and as a pretense you make long prayers. Therefore you will receive greater condemnation.*

"But woe to you, scribes and Pharisees, hypocrites! Because you shut up the Kingdom of Heaven against men; for you don't enter in yourselves, neither do you allow those who are entering in to enter. Woe to you, scribes and Pharisees, hypocrites! For you travel around by and land to make one proselyte; and when he becomes one, you make him twice as much a son of Gehenna as yourselves.

"Woe to you, you blind guides, who say, 'Whoever swears by the temple, it is nothing; but whoever swears by the gold of the temple, he is obligated.' You blind fools! For which is greater, the gold, or the temple that sanctifies the gold? 'Whoever swears by the altar, it is nothing; but whoever swears by the gift that is on it, he is obligated?' You blind fools! For which is greater, the gift, or the altar that sanctifies the gift? He therefore who swears by the altar, swears by it, and by everything on it. He who swears by the temple, swears by it, and by him who has been living in it. He who swears by heaven, swears by the throne of God, and by him who sits on it.

"Woe to you, scribes and Pharisees, hypocrites! For you tithe mint, dill, and cumin, and have left undone the weightier matters of the law: justice, mercy, and faith. But you ought to have done these, and not to have left the other undone. You blind guides, who strain out a gnat, and swallow a camel!

"Woe to you, scribes and Pharisees, hypocrites! For you clean the outside of the cup and of the platter, but within they are full of extortion and unrighteousness. You blind Pharisee, first clean the inside of the cup and of the platter, that its outside may become clean also.

"Woe to you, scribes and Pharisees, hypocrites! For you are like whitened tombs, which outwardly appear beautiful, but inwardly are full of dead men's bones, and of all uncleanness. Even so you also outwardly appear righteous to men, but inwardly you are full of hypocrisy and iniquity.

"Woe to you, scribes and Pharisees, hypocrites! For you build the tombs of the prophets, and decorate the tombs of the righteous, and say, 'If we had lived in the days of our fathers, we wouldn't have been partakers with them in the blood of the prophets.'

*"Therefore you testify to yourselves that you are children of those who killed the prophets. Fill up, then, the measure of your fathers. You serpents, you offspring of vipers, how will you escape the judgment of Gehenna? Therefore behold, I send to you prophets, wise men, and scribes. Some of them you will kill and crucify; and some of them you will scourge in your synagogues, and persecute from city to city; that on you may come all the righteous blood shed on the earth, from the blood of righteous Abel to the blood of Zachariah son of Barachiah, whom you killed between the sanctuary and the altar.*

*"Most certainly I tell you, all these things will come upon this generation.*

*"Jerusalem, Jerusalem, who kills the prophets, and stones those who are sent to her! How often I would have gathered your children together, even as a hen gathers her chicks under her wings, and you would not!*

*"Behold, your house is left to you desolate. For I tell you, you will not see me from now on, until you say, 'Blessed is he who comes in the name of the Lord!'"*

## PROPHECIES IN THIS CHAPTER

**2 Chronicles 24:19** - Yet he sent prophets to them, to bring them again to The Lord; and they testified against them: but they would not give ear.

**2 Chronicles 36:15-16** - The Lord, the God of their fathers, sent to them by his messengers, rising up early and sending, because he had compassion on his people, and on his dwelling place: but they mocked the messengers of God, and despised his words, and scoffed at his prophets, until The Lord's wrath arose against his people, until there was no remedy.

**Nehemiah 9:26** - "Nevertheless they were disobedient, and rebelled against you, and cast your law behind their back, and killed your prophets that testified against them to turn them again to you, and they committed awful blasphemies.

**Jeremiah 12:7** - I have forsaken my house, I have cast off my heritage; I have given the dearly beloved of my soul into the hand of her enemies.

**Matthew 23:34** - Therefore behold, I send to you prophets, wise men, and scribes. Some of them you will kill and crucify; and some of them you will scourge in your synagogues, and persecute from city to city;

**Matthew 23:37** - "Jerusalem, Jerusalem, who kills the prophets, and stones those who are sent to her! How often I would have gathered your children together, even as a hen gathers her chicks under her wings, and you would not!

**Matthew 23:39** - For I tell you, you will not see me from now on, until you say, 'Blessed is he who comes in the name of the Lord!'"

## WHY THESE PROPHECIES ARE IMPORTANT

Since each of the prophecies in this chapter speak of Israel's rejection of Jesus as the Messiah, I will not speak of each of them individually, but rather talk about them as a group. Israel had rejected other prophets along the way, and it was foretold they would reject the dearly beloved of God, who is Jesus.

Even to this day, many Jews, especially the religious leaders, cannot see Jesus as the Messiah. Jews for Jesus is one organization that helps Jewish people understand Jesus is indeed the Messiah, if they have eyes to see and ears to hear.

It is a hard concept for them to accept Jesus, but their rejection of Jesus is to be expected, because it was prophesied. God said they would reject His beloved, and indeed the Jewish people reject Jesus.

As we had mentioned earlier in this study, if they accepted Jesus as the Messiah, then it would be an indicator that Jesus was perhaps not the Messiah.

These prophecies about the rejection of Jesus give us an added measure of confidence. Jesus is the Messiah, the Chosen One for us to follow, because He was and still is rejected by so many.

## WHAT STANDS OUT IN THESE PROPHECIES TO YOU?

_____
_____
_____
_____
_____
_____
_____

## WHAT DO YOU THINK?

➢ In what circumstances do you see people laying expectations on others, where they are no better, or not willing, to lift a finger to help others?

_____
_____
_____
_____
_____
_____
_____

➤ If you have only one true Teacher (Christ) and one true Father (God), how can you best learn what they teach and their expectations of you? In what ways are their expectations and teachings different from your earthly teachers and earthly father?

___

➤ How do church leaders shut up the kingdom of heaven and keep others from entering?

___

➤ What are some weightier matters in your life, on which God might want you to focus?

___

➤ What is inside of you which needs cleaning in order for you to be more Godly inside and out?

___

➢ Why do people often ignore God's messengers, mock them, or murder them? Why do so many people pay no heed to God's Word or His warnings?

_____
_____
_____
_____
_____
_____
_____

# ACTION ITEM:

Write a "Woe to you, Religious Hypocrites," statement describing the sinful nature of those who practice religion on Sundays, but don't have any relationship with God in their day-to-day lives:

_____
_____
_____
_____
_____
_____
_____
_____
_____
_____
_____
_____

Consider what you've written and reflect on the Greatest Commandment to "love the Lord your God with all your heart, soul, strength, and mind." Is there anything you need to change in your personal relationship with God? If so, set your mind on changing yourself through prayer, partnership with God, and by exercising self-control.

# WHAT'S NEXT?

In the next chapter, Jesus tells us what to expect at the end of this age, and He tells us with clarity exactly what will happen. Jesus also tells us what we should and shouldn't do at that time.

The next chapter is worth reading multiple times. It will give you clarity about what to expect and how to stay true to the Lord through the end times.

Highlight the specific directives Jesus gives, especially when he says "don't" do this, "do" that, or gives a warning of what to be aware. Wherever you see something you should or shouldn't do, make notes for yourself, so you won't easily be led astray!

# MATTHEW 24

Jesus went out from the temple, and was going on his way. His disciples came to him to show him the buildings of the temple. But he answered them, *"You see all of these things, don't you? Most certainly I tell you, there will not be left here one stone on another, that will not be thrown down."*

As he sat on the Mount of Olives, the disciples came to him privately, saying, "Tell us, when will these things be? What is the sign of your coming, and of the end of the age?"

Jesus answered them, *"Be careful that no one leads you astray. For many will come in my name, saying, 'I am the Christ,' and will lead many astray. You will hear of wars and rumors of wars. See that you aren't troubled, for all this must happen, but the end is not yet. For nation will rise against nation, and kingdom against kingdom; and there will be famines, plagues, and earthquakes in various places.*

*"But all these things are the beginning of birth pains. Then they will deliver you up to oppression, and will kill you. You will be hated by all of the nations for my name's sake. Then many will stumble, and will deliver up one another, and will hate one another. Many false prophets will arise, and will lead many astray. Because iniquity will be multiplied, the love of many will grow cold.*

"But he who endures to the end will be saved. This Good News of the Kingdom will be preached in the whole world for a testimony to all the nations, and then the end will come.

"When, therefore, you see the abomination of desolation, which was spoken of through Daniel the prophet, standing in the holy place (let the reader understand), then let those who are in Judea flee to the mountains. Let him who is on the housetop not go down to take out the things that are in his house. Let him who is in the field not return back to get his clothes. But woe to those who are with child and to nursing mothers in those days! Pray that your flight will not be in the winter, nor on a Sabbath, for then there will be great suffering, such as has not been from the beginning of the world until now, no, nor ever will be. Unless those days had been shortened, no flesh would have been saved. But for the sake of the chosen ones, those days will be shortened.

"Then if any man tells you, 'Behold, here is the Christ,' or, 'There,' don't believe it. For there will arise false christs, and false prophets, and they will show great signs and wonders, so as to lead astray, if possible, even the chosen ones.

"Behold, I have told you beforehand. If therefore they tell you, 'Behold, he is in the wilderness,' don't go out; or 'Behold, he is in the inner rooms,' don't believe it. For as the lightning flashes from the east, and is seen even to the west, so will the coming of the Son of Man be. For wherever the carcass is, that is where the vultures gather together. But immediately after the suffering of those days, the sun will be darkened, the moon will not give its light, the stars will fall from the sky, and the powers of the heavens will be shaken; and then the sign of the Son of Man will appear in the sky.

"Then all the tribes of the earth will mourn, and they will see the Son of Man coming on the clouds of the sky with power and great glory. He will send out his angels with a great sound of a trumpet, and they will gather together his chosen ones from the four winds, from one end of the sky to the other. "Now from the fig tree learn this parable. When its branch has now become tender, and produces its leaves, you know that the summer is near. Even so you also, when you see all these things, know that it is near, even at the doors.

"Most certainly I tell you, this generation will not pass away, until all these things are accomplished. Heaven and earth will pass away, but my words will not pass away.

"But no one knows of that day and hour, not even the angels of heaven, but my Father only.

"As the days of Noah were, so will the coming of the Son of Man be. For as in those days which were before the flood they were eating and drinking, marrying and giving in marriage, until the day that Noah entered into the ship, and they didn't know until the flood came, and took them all away, so will the coming of the Son of Man be. Then two men will be in the field: one will be taken and one will be left. Two women will be grinding at the mill: one will be taken and one will be left. Watch therefore, for you don't know in what hour your Lord comes. But know this, that if the master of the house had known in what watch of the night the thief was coming, he would have watched, and would not have allowed his house to be broken into. Therefore also be ready, for in an hour that you don't expect, the Son of Man will come.

"Who then is the faithful and wise servant, whom his lord has set over his household, to give them their food in due season? Blessed is that servant whom his lord finds doing so when he comes. Most certainly I tell you that he will set him over all that he has. But if that evil servant should say in his heart, 'My lord is delaying his coming,' and begins to beat his fellow servants, and eat and drink with the drunkards, the lord of that servant will come in a day when he doesn't expect it, and in an hour when he doesn't know it, and will cut him in pieces, and appoint his portion with the hypocrites. That is where the weeping and grinding of teeth will be."

# PROPHECIES IN THIS CHAPTER

**Daniel 9:24-27** – To reread and review this prophecy, see chapter 20.

**Matthew 24:2** – "But he answered them, 'You see all of these things, don't you? Most certainly I tell you, there will not be left here one stone on another, that will not be thrown down.'" (Jesus prophecies the destruction of the temple, which occurred in 70 A.D.)

**Daniel 9:25** – Know therefore and discern, that from the going out of the commandment to restore and to build Jerusalem to the Anointed One, the prince, shall be seven weeks, and sixty-two weeks: it shall be built again, with street and moat, even in troubled times.

**Daniel 9:27** – He shall make a firm covenant with many for one week: and in the middle of the week he shall cause the sacrifice and the offering to cease; and on the wing of abominations shall come one who makes desolate; and even to the full end, and that determined, shall wrath be poured out on the desolate.

**Daniel 11:31** – Forces shall stand on his part, and they shall profane the sanctuary, even the fortress, and shall take away the continual burnt offering, and they shall set up the abomination that makes desolate.

**Matthew 24:14** – This Good News of the Kingdom will be preached in the whole world for a testimony to all the nations, and then the end will come.

**Matthew 24:15-31** – Jesus prophesies: "When, therefore, you see the abomination of desolation, which was spoken of through Daniel the prophet, standing in the holy place (let the reader understand), then let those who are in Judea flee to the mountains. Let him who is on the housetop not go down to take out things that are in his house. Let him who is in the field not return back to get his clothes. But woe to those who are with child and to nursing mothers in those days! Pray that your flight will not be in the winter, nor on a Sabbath, for then there will be great oppression, such as has not been from the beginning of the world until now, no, nor ever will be. Unless those days had been shortened, no flesh would have been saved. But for the sake of the chosen ones, those days will be shortened.

"Then if any man tells you, 'Behold, here is the Christ,' or, 'There,' don't believe it. For there will arise false christs, and false prophets, and they will show great signs and wonders, so as to lead astray, if possible, even the chosen ones.

"Behold, I have told you beforehand. If therefore they tell you, 'Behold, he is in the wilderness,' don't go out; 'Behold, he is in the inner rooms,' don't believe it. For as the lightning flashes from the east, and is seen even to the west, so will be the coming of the Son of Man. For wherever the carcass is, there is where the vultures gather together. But immediately after the oppression of those days, the sun will be darkened, the moon will not give its light, the stars will fall from the sky, and the powers of the heavens will be shaken; and then the sign of the Son of Man will appear in the sky. Then all the tribes of the earth will mourn, and they will see the Son of Man coming on the clouds of the sky with power and great glory. He will send out his angels with a great sound of a trumpet, and they will gather together his chosen ones from the four winds, from one end of the sky to the other."

## WHY THESE PROPHECIES ARE IMPORTANT

In Daniel 11:31, Daniel prophecies the destruction of the Temple. In Matthew 24:2 and Matthew 24:15-31, Jesus prophecies the destruction of the temple also. We know the destruction occurred in 70 A.D., so these were accurate prophesies from Daniel and Jesus. We previously discussed the importance of this event Chapter 20, if you'd like to look back and refresh your memory.

In Matthew 24:14, Jesus also prophecies the gospel message will be preached to the whole world, then the end will come. We know the gospel message is spreading throughout the world and has been ever since Jesus lived on earth. When the end comes, everyone will know, without a doubt, Jesus is the Messiah and all of His prophecies are accurate.

## WHAT STANDS OUT IN THESE PROPHECIES TO YOU?

_____
_____
_____
_____
_____
_____

# WHAT DO YOU THINK?

➢ Based on Jesus's description of the end times, what signs of the coming of the end of the age do you see in the world today?

_____
_____
_____
_____
_____
_____

➢ What do people's relationships look like when their love for each other grows cold? Where do you see a lack of love in today's society?

_____
_____
_____
_____
_____
_____

➢ Jesus tells us plainly that false prophets will lead people astray. How will Jesus's teachings keep you from being led astray by false prophets?

_____
_____
_____
_____
_____
_____

➢ Jesus describes what will happen when he returns to earth. It will not be a quiet, nor secret event. Write down all of the things Jesus says you will see and hear, if you are still alive when he returns.

_____
_____
_____
_____
_____
_____

➤ Jesus said His words will never pass away. They are still being shared 2,000 years after He lived on Earth. What makes Jesus's teachings relevant in every generation, including in your generation?

_____
_____
_____
_____
_____
_____

➤ What do you think Jesus expects His faithful, wise servants to be doing as we wait for His return?

_____
_____
_____
_____
_____
_____
_____

# ACTION ITEM:

In Jesus' description of the end times, He says the love of many will grow cold. Think of some ways you can express greater love to and for the people in your life. Decide upon something loving you can do for someone else, then do it. Begin practicing the expression of love to others as opportunities present themselves. What will you do to show love to someone else this week?

_____
_____
_____
_____

# WHAT'S NEXT?

The next chapter is a continuation of Jesus teaching the multitude of people. He talks about what the Kingdom of Heaven is like in two additional illustrations. In these descriptions, Jesus includes examples of what judgement will be like. Pay close attention to the judgments made against the lazy and careless people in Jesus' stories. Consider what you can learn from these examples, and reflect upon how you might want to change your own behaviors, so you won't be deemed lazy or careless.

# MATTHEW 25

"Then the Kingdom of Heaven will be like ten virgins, who took their lamps, and went out to meet the bridegroom. Five of them were foolish, and five were wise. Those who were foolish, when they took their lamps, took no oil with them, but the wise took oil in their vessels with their lamps. Now while the bridegroom delayed, they all slumbered and slept. But at midnight there was a cry, 'Behold! The bridegroom is coming! Come out to meet him!' Then all those virgins arose, and trimmed their lamps. The foolish said to the wise, 'Give us some of your oil, for our lamps are going out.' But the wise answered, saying, 'What if there isn't enough for us and you? You go rather to those who sell, and buy for yourselves.' While they went away to buy, the bridegroom came, and those who were ready went in with him to the wedding feast, and the door was shut. Afterward the other virgins also came, saying, 'Lord, Lord, open to us.' But he answered, 'Most certainly I tell you, I don't know you.' Watch therefore, for you don't know the day nor the hour in which the Son of Man is coming.

"For it is like a man, going into another country, who called his own servants, and entrusted his goods to them.

"To one he gave five talents, to another two, to another one; to each according to his own ability.

"Then he went on his journey.

"Immediately he who received the five talents went and traded with them, and made another five talents. In the same way, he also who got the two gained another two. But he who received the one talent went away and dug in the earth, and hid his lord's money.

"Now after a long time the lord of those servants came, and reconciled accounts with them. He who received the five talents came and brought another five talents, saying, 'Lord, you delivered to me five talents. Behold, I have gained another five talents in addition to them.'

"His lord said to him, 'Well done, good and faithful servant. You have been faithful over a few things, I will set you over many things. Enter into the joy of your lord.'

"He also who got the two talents came and said, 'Lord, you delivered to me two talents. Behold, I have gained another two talents in addition to them.'

"His lord said to him, 'Well done, good and faithful servant. You have been faithful over a few things, I will set you over many things. Enter into the joy of your lord.'

"He also who had received the one talent came and said, 'Lord, I knew you that you are a hard man, reaping where you didn't sow, and gathering where you didn't scatter. I was afraid, and went away and hid your talent in the earth. Behold, you have what is yours.'

"But his lord answered him, 'You wicked and slothful servant. You knew that I reap where I didn't sow, and gather where I didn't scatter. You ought therefore to have deposited my money with the bankers, and at my coming I should have received back my own with interest.

"Take away therefore the talent from him, and give it to him who has the ten talents. For to everyone who has will be given, and he will have abundance, but from him who doesn't have, even that which he has will be taken away. Throw out the unprofitable servant into the outer darkness, where there will be weeping and gnashing of teeth.'

"But when the Son of Man comes in his glory, and all the holy angels with him, then he will sit on the throne of his glory. Before him all the nations will be gathered, and he will separate them one from another, as a shepherd separates the sheep from the goats.

*"He will set the sheep on his right hand, but the goats on the left. Then the King will tell those on his right hand, 'Come, blessed of my Father, inherit the Kingdom prepared for you from the foundation of the world; for I was hungry, and you gave me food to eat. I was thirsty, and you gave me drink. I was a stranger, and you took me in. I was naked, and you clothed me. I was sick, and you visited me. I was in prison, and you came to me.',*

*"Then the righteous will answer him, saying, 'Lord, when did we see you hungry, and feed you; or thirsty, and give you a drink? When did we see you as a stranger, and take you in; or naked, and clothe you? When did we see you sick, or in prison, and come to you?'*

*"The King will answer them, 'Most certainly I tell you, because you did it to one of the least of these my brothers, you did it to me.' Then he will say also to those on the left hand, 'Depart from me, you cursed, into the eternal fire which is prepared for the devil and his angels; for I was hungry, and you didn't give me food to eat; I was thirsty, and you gave me no drink; I was a stranger, and you didn't take me in; naked, and you didn't clothe me; sick, and in prison, and you didn't visit me.'*

*"Then they will also answer, saying, 'Lord, when did we see you hungry, or thirsty, or a stranger, or naked, or sick, or in prison, and didn't help you?'*

*"Then he will answer them, saying, 'Most certainly I tell you, because you didn't do it to one of the least of these, you didn't do it to me.' These will go away into eternal punishment, but the righteous into eternal life."*

# PROPHECIES IN THIS CHAPTER

**Matthew 25:31-46** – "But when the Son of Man comes in his glory, and all the holy angels with him, then he will sit on the throne of his glory. Before him all the nations will be gathered, and he will separate them one from another, as a shepherd separates the sheep from the goats. He will set the sheep on his right hand, but the goats on the left. Then the King will tell those on his right hand, 'Come, blessed of my Father, inherit the Kingdom prepared for you from the foundation of the world; for I was hungry, and you gave me food to eat. I was thirsty, and you gave me drink. I was a stranger, and you took me in. I was naked, and you clothed me. I was sick, and you visited me. I was in prison, and you came to me.'

"Then the righteous will answer him, saying, 'Lord, when did we see you hungry, and feed you; or thirsty, and give you a drink? When did we see you as a stranger, and take you in; or naked, and clothe you? When did we see you sick, or in prison, and come to you?'

"The King will answer them, 'Most certainly I tell you, because you did it to one of the least of these my brothers , you did it to me.'

Then he will say also to those on the left hand, 'Depart from me, you cursed, into the eternal fire which is prepared for the devil and his angels; for I was hungry, and you didn't give me food to eat; I was thirsty, and you gave me no drink; I was a stranger, and you didn't take me in; naked, and you didn't clothe me; sick, and in prison, and you didn't visit me.'

"Then they will also answer, saying, 'Lord, when did we see you hungry, or thirsty, or a stranger, or naked, or sick, or in prison, and didn't help you?'

"Then he will answer them, saying, 'Most certainly I tell you, because you didn't do it to one of the least of these, you didn't do it to me.' These will go away into eternal punishment, but the righteous into eternal life.'"

**Daniel 12:2** – Many of those who sleep in the dust of the earth shall awake, some to everlasting life, and some to shame and everlasting contempt.

## WHY THESE PROPHECIES ARE IMPORTANT

In this chapter, Jesus tells of His actions at the judgement after his second coming to Earth. The related prophecies are important, because when these events take place, just as Jesus has described, then it will be crystal clear Jesus is the one and only true Messiah. It will be as was foretold by God's prophets hundreds of years before his first coming, and thousands of years before his second coming!

No other faith has the backing of so many prophecies coming true, as foretold by God's prophets in the Old Testament scriptures, to give confirmation their beliefs are from the one true God.

Here we also see that Daniel 2:12 refers to the last day on Earth, which will come with the events described by Jesus in the separation of the sheep from the goats.

## WHAT STANDS OUT IN THESE PROPHECIES TO YOU?

# WHAT DO YOU THINK?

➢ What kinds of things would you be wise to do, in order to be prepared when Jesus returns to Earth?

_____
_____
_____
_____
_____

➢ What talents has God given you? How can you use your talents to serve God and other people?

_____
_____
_____
_____
_____

➢ Based on the three servants and their talents, at the end of your life, what do you think God will be looking for when He examines you to see how you have invested your gifts and talents?

_____
_____
_____
_____
_____

➢ The servant who hid his talent didn't do anything meaningful or helpful. He was punished with the wicked people. Why is it sinful to do nothing worthwhile with your gifts and talents?

_____
_____
_____
_____
_____

➢ When Jesus separates good from bad, we'll be sorted as sheep and goats. What are some things you believe Jesus expects you to do, if you wish to be sorted as a sheep going to heaven?

___

➢ Jesus is clear about heaven and the existence of eternal punishment. Why do you think people choose to believe God would never send anyone to hell? How does a person's belief about hell affect their behavior in life?

___

# ACTION ITEM:

God gives us gifts and talents to help other people, whether we're helping one person or many people. You can help someone in some way. Choose one gift or talent God has freely given you, and think of a way you'd like to share your gift(s) with others. Find an opportunity to share your gift by considering opportunities in your life. Write your plan below, then do what you've planned.

___

# WHAT'S NEXT?

In the next chapter, the end of Jesus on Earth is at hand. Jesus and His disciples share a Passover meal, and one of the disciples turns against Jesus. Jesus pleads with God, His Heavenly Father, to avoid the torture that lies ahead, and things seem to go badly from there.

As you read, keep in mind these harsh events were part of God's foretold plan all along. God told us what would happen hundreds of years beforehand. These events are prophesies fulfilled, in which we can see who is the true Messiah. Even though we know these are necessary events, our hearts ache for Jesus, for He is a good and wise friend at this point in our study.

# MATTHEW 26

When Jesus had finished all these words, he said to his disciples, *"You know that after two days the Passover is coming, and the Son of Man will be delivered up to be crucified."*

Then the chief priests, the scribes, and the elders of the people were gathered together in the court of the high priest, who was called Caiaphas. They took counsel together that they might take Jesus by deceit, and kill him. But they said, "Not during the feast, lest a riot occur among the people."

Now when Jesus was in Bethany, in the house of Simon the leper, a woman came to him having an alabaster jar of very expensive ointment, and she poured it on his head as he sat at the table. But when his disciples saw this, they were indignant, saying, "Why this waste? For this ointment might have been sold for much, and given to the poor."

However, knowing this, Jesus said to them, *"Why do you trouble the woman? She has done a good work for me. For you always have the poor with you; but you don't always have me. For in pouring this ointment on my body, she did it to prepare me for burial. Most certainly I tell you, wherever this Good News is preached in the whole world, what this woman has done will also be spoken of as a memorial of her.*"

Then one of the twelve, who was called Judas Iscariot, went to the chief priests, and said, "What are you willing to give me, that I should deliver him to you?" They weighed out for him thirty pieces of silver. From that time he sought opportunity to betray him.

Now on the first day of unleavened bread, the disciples came to Jesus, saying to him, "Where do you want us to prepare for you to eat the Passover?"

He said, *"Go into the city to a certain person, and tell him, 'The Teacher says, My time is at hand. I will keep the Passover at your house with my disciples.'"*

The disciples did as Jesus commanded them, and they prepared the Passover. Now when evening had come, he was reclining at the table with the twelve disciples. As they were eating, he said, *"Most certainly I tell you that one of you will betray me."*

They were exceedingly sorrowful, and each began to ask him, "It isn't me, is it, Lord?"

He answered, *"He who dipped his hand with me in the dish will betray me. The Son of Man goes, even as it is written of him, but woe to that man through whom the Son of Man is betrayed! It would be better for that man if he had not been born."*

Judas, who betrayed him, answered, "It isn't me, is it, Rabbi?"

He said to him, *"You said it."*

As they were eating, Jesus took bread, gave thanks for it, and broke it. He gave to the disciples, and said, *"Take, eat; this is my body."* He took the cup, gave thanks, and gave to them, saying, *"All of you drink it, for this is my blood of the new covenant, which is poured out for many for the remission of sins. But I tell you that I will not drink of this fruit of the vine from now on, until that day when I drink it anew with you in my Father's Kingdom."* When they had sung a hymn, they went out to the Mount of Olives.

Then Jesus said to them, *"All of you will be made to stumble because of me tonight, for it is written, I will strike the shepherd, and the sheep of the flock will be scattered.' But after I am raised up, I will go before you into Galilee."*

But Peter answered him, "Even if all will be made to stumble because of you, I will never be made to stumble."

Jesus said to him, *"Most certainly I tell you that tonight, before the rooster crows, you will deny me three times."*

Peter said to him, "Even if I must die with you, I will not deny you." All of the disciples also said likewise.

Then Jesus came with them to a place called Gethsemane, and said to his disciples, *"Sit here, while I go there and pray."* He took with him Peter and the two sons of Zebedee, and began to be sorrowful and severely troubled. Then he said to them, *"My soul is exceedingly sorrowful, even to death. Stay here, and watch with me."* He went forward a little, fell on his face, and prayed, saying, *"My Father, if it is possible, let this cup pass away from me; nevertheless, not what I desire, but what you desire."*

He came to the disciples, and found them sleeping, and said to Peter, *"What, couldn't you watch with me for one hour? Watch and pray, that you don't enter into temptation. The spirit indeed is willing, but the flesh is weak."*

Again, a second time he went away, and prayed, saying, *"My Father, if this cup can't pass away from me unless I drink it, your desire be done."* He came again and found them sleeping, for their eyes were heavy. He left them again, went away, and prayed a third time, saying the same words. Then he came to his disciples, and said to them, *"Sleep on now, and take your rest. Behold, the hour is at hand, and the Son of Man is betrayed into the hands of sinners. Arise, let's be going. Behold, he who betrays me is at hand."*

While he was still speaking, behold, Judas, one of the twelve, came, and with him a great multitude with swords and clubs, from the chief priests and elders of the people. Now he who betrayed him gave them a sign, saying, "Whoever I kiss, he is the one. Seize him."

Immediately he came to Jesus, and said, "Hail, Rabbi!" and kissed him.

Jesus said to him, *"Friend, why are you here?"* Then they came and laid hands on Jesus, and took him. Behold, one of those who were with Jesus stretched out his hand, and drew his sword, and struck the servant of the high priest, and struck off his ear.

Then Jesus said to him, *"Put your sword back into its place, for all those who take the sword will die by the sword. Or do you think that I couldn't ask my Father, and he would even now send me more than twelve legions of angels? How then would the Scriptures be fulfilled that it must be so?"*

In that hour Jesus said to the multitudes, *"Have you come out as against a robber with swords and clubs to seize me? I sat daily in the temple teaching, and you didn't arrest me. But all this has happened that the Scriptures of the prophets might be fulfilled."*

Then all the disciples left him and fled. Those who had taken Jesus led him away to Caiaphas the high priest, where the scribes and the elders were gathered together.

But Peter followed him from a distance, to the court of the high priest, and entered in and sat with the officers, to see the end.

Now the chief priests, the elders, and the whole council sought false testimony against Jesus, that they might put him to death; and they found none. Even though many false witnesses came forward, they found none. But at last two false witnesses came forward, and said, "This man said, 'I am able to destroy the temple of God, and to build it in three days.'"

The high priest stood up, and said to him, "Have you no answer? What is this that these testify against you?" But Jesus held his peace.

The high priest answered him, "I adjure you by the living God, that you tell us whether you are the Christ, the Son of God."

Jesus said to him, *"You have said it. Nevertheless, I tell you, after this you will see the Son of Man sitting at the right hand of Power, and coming on the clouds of the sky."*

Then the high priest tore his clothing, saying, "He has spoken blasphemy! Why do we need any more witnesses? Behold, now you have heard his blasphemy. What do you think?"

They answered, "He is worthy of death!" Then they spat in his face and beat him with their fists, and some slapped him, saying, "Prophesy to us, you Christ! Who hit you?"

Now Peter was sitting outside in the court, and a maid came to him, saying, "You were also with Jesus, the Galilean!"

But he denied it before them all, saying, "I don't know what you are talking about."

When he had gone out onto the porch, someone else saw him, and said to those who were there, "This man also was with Jesus of Nazareth."

Again he denied it with an oath, "I don't know the man."

After a little while those who stood by came and said to Peter, "Surely you are also one of them, for your speech makes you known."

Then he began to curse and to swear, "I don't know the man!"

Immediately the rooster crowed. Peter remembered the word which Jesus had said to him, "*Before the rooster crows, you will deny me three times.*" Then he went out and wept bitterly.

# PROPHECIES IN THIS CHAPTER

**Zechariah 11:12-13** – "I said to them, "If you think it best, give me my wages; and if not, keep them." So they weighed for my wages thirty pieces of silver. The Lord said to me, "Throw it to the potter, the handsome price that I was valued at by them!" I took the thirty pieces of silver, and threw them to the potter, in The Lord's house."

**Isaiah 52:13-53:12** – To Read this full text, see the bonus chapter after chapter 28.

**Jeremiah 31:31** – "Behold, the days come, says The Lord, that I will make a new covenant with the house of Israel, and with the house of Judah"

**Matthew 26:2** - "You know that after two days the Passover is coming, and the Son of Man will be delivered up to be crucified."

**Matthew 26:20-25** – [20] "Now when evening had come, he was reclining at the table with the twelve disciples. As they were eating, he said, 'Most certainly I tell you that one of you will betray me.'

"They were exceedingly sorrowful, and each began to ask him, 'It isn't me, is it, Lord?'

"He answered, 'He who dipped his hand with me in the dish, the same will betray me. The Son of Man goes, even as it is written of him, but woe to that man through whom the Son of Man is betrayed! It would be better for that man if he had not been born.'

"Judas, who betrayed him, answered, "It isn't me, is it, Rabbi?"

"He said to him, 'You said it.'"

**Matthew 26:29** – "But I tell you that I will not drink of this fruit of the vine from now on, until that day when I drink it anew with you in my Father's Kingdom."

**Matthew 26:31** – "Then Jesus said to them, 'All of you will be made to stumble because of me tonight, for it is written, 'I will strike the shepherd, and the sheep of the flock will be scattered.'" (fulfilled in Matthew 26:56)

**Matthew 26:32** – "But after I am raised up, I will go before you into Galilee."

**Matthew 26:34** – "Jesus said to him, 'Most certainly I tell you that tonight, before the rooster crows, you will deny me three times.'"

**Isaiah 50:6** - I gave my back to those who beat me, and my cheeks to those who plucked off the hair. I didn't hide my face from shame and spitting.

**Psalm 41:9** - Yes, my own familiar friend, in whom I trusted, who ate bread with me, has lifted up his heel against me.

**Psalm 55:12-13** - For it was not an enemy who insulted me, then I could have endured it. Neither was it he who hated me who raised himself up against me, then I would have hidden myself from him. But it was you, a man like me, my companion, and my familiar friend.

**Psalm 2:2** - The kings of the earth take a stand, and the rulers take counsel together, against The Lord, and against his Anointed.

**Psalm 27:12** - Don't deliver me over to the desire of my adversaries, for false witnesses have risen up against me, such as breathe out cruelty.

**Psalm 88:8** - You have taken my friends from me. You have made me an abomination to them. I am confined, and I can't escape.

**Psalm 88:18** - You have put lover and friend far from me, and my friends into darkness.

**Proverbs 9:5-6** - "Come, eat some of my bread, Drink some of the wine which I have mixed! Leave your simple ways, and live. Walk in the way of understanding."

**Zechariah 13:7** - "Awake, sword, against my shepherd, and against the man who is close to me," says The Lord of Armies. "Strike the shepherd, and the sheep will be scattered; and I will turn my hand against the little ones."

# WHY THESE PROPHECIES ARE IMPORTANT

This and the next two chapters are the culmination of Matthew's book about the life of Jesus. In these final three chapters we see numerous prophecies being fulfilled, often with great detail.

For example, Zechariah 11:12-13 speaks of the 30 pieces of silver which Judas received for betraying Jesus. In his guilt, Judas returned the 30 pieces of silver, just as was prophesied by Zechariah hundreds of years earlier.

In Matthew 26, where Jesus is conducting the first communion, He refers to blood of the New Covenant, which is poured out for many for the remission of sins. This new covenant was prophesied in Jeremiah 31:31. It was told there would be a new covenant with Israel and the house of Judah. The new covenant is based on belief in Jesus as the Son of God and for His remission of sins, paid for by Jesus.

In this chapter of Matthew, we also see several instances in which Jesus prophesies about events which will happen in the very near future. He began by saying one of the disciples would betray him, and the betraying disciple was Judas.

Jesus says he will not drink of the wine again until he drinks it in the Father's Kingdom. He also tells His disciples He will be delivered up to be crucified.

Jesus prophecies all of the flock of the sheep will be scattered, meaning the disciples would all go in different directions, when Jesus was taken into custody.

Jesus even told Peter he would deny Jesus three times. Peter was insistent he would not, but we see Peter did exactly as Jesus prophesied he would.

And one of the most confusing things Jesus prophesied at the time, was saying after He is raised up He will go before the disciples into Galilee. Before Jesus' death, the disciples didn't grasp that Jesus would be killed, then Resurrected. Thus, the disciples probably didn't understand this prophecy clearly.

Each of the prophecies Jesus spoke in Matthew 26 came to pass exactly as Jesus said they would. Here again, we know Jesus had the spiritual ability to be able to accurately speak of future events.

Isaiah 50 is a prophecy referencing the way the Messiah would be treated. As He is taken into custody in this chapter, we see Jesus is passive, regardless of the beatings, slapping, hitting, and spitting. Because Jesus was treated so badly, we can clearly see this prophecy applies to Jesus.

Psalm 41:9 and Psalm 55:12-13 say the Messiah will be betrayed by a familiar friend, with whom He dined and trusted. Judas, who betrayed Jesus, was a familiar friend.

These prophecies, with their details, make it all the more clear it's extremely unlikely the Messiah is anyone else in history. There is no one else who lived before the destruction of the temple in Jerusalem, who comes anywhere close to fitting the Biblical description of the Messiah. Statistically speaking, when it comes to the fulfillment of prophesies, it seems clear Jesus is the One and only Messiah.

The remaining prophecy verses in Psalm 2, Psalm 27, Psalm 28, Proverbs 9, and Zechariah 13 relate to the delivery of Jesus over to His adversaries. They speak about the Messiah being abandoned by His friends, the disciples. I don't think we need to explain each of these verses in detail, because the reference to what is happening to Jesus in Matthew 26 is fairly clear. Suffice it to say, these descriptions of the Messiah, as one who is treated badly by worldly and religious leaders, who is abandoned by those closest to him, all point toward Jesus as the One and only true Son of God.

# WHAT STANDS OUT IN THESE PROPHECIES TO YOU?

_____
_____
_____
_____
_____
_____
_____
_____

# WHAT DO YOU THINK?

➢ The high priest and his Council schemed and deceived in order to kill Jesus, because they hated Him. If Jesus were alive today, who do you think would want to kill Him and why?

_____
_____
_____
_____
_____
_____
_____
_____

➢ We deserve the death penalty for our sins, but Jesus gave his life for us instead. He gave us a clean slate. What will you do differently in the future to live a better life, since Jesus paid your penalty?

_____
_____
_____
_____
_____
_____
_____
_____

➢ As one of Jesus's followers, what would you do and say, if you were there when Jesus was arrested? What kinds of fears and emotions would you be feeling?

___

➢ Using Jesus as an example, what are some reasons God may deny some of our prayer requests? Why is it difficult for us to accept God's will when things don't go as we have prayed they would?

___

➢ What are some reasons Jesus was willing to go to His death, even though He could have saved Himself? Why was Jesus willing to die and pay the death penalty for all of our sins?

___

➢ Why didn't Jesus try to defend himself against the accusations and abuse He faced?

___

## ACTION ITEM:

In the Passover meal, Jesus took bread, gave thanks, and broke the bread. He gave it to the disciples, and said, *"Take, eat; this is my body."* He took the cup, gave thanks, and gave it to them, saying, *"All of you drink it, for this is my blood of the new covenant, which is poured out for many for the remission of sins."*

Pour yourself a small cup of wine or grape juice and get a small piece of bread (if you're not allergic to either). Sit for a moment and reflect on the sacrifice Jesus made when He gave His life, so you and I won't receive the punishment we deserve for our sins. Examine your heart for unconfessed sin, and ask Jesus to forgive you.

Say a prayer of thanksgiving that you are forgiven, then eat the bread and drink the wine while remembering Jesus.

## WHAT'S NEXT?

In the next chapter, Jesus fulfills His purpose for coming to earth in the cruelest of circumstances for an innocent man. As you read, consider what would be your thoughts and feelings, if you were an eye-witness to these events. Consider the price Jesus paid by laying down His life for us in order to save us and demonstrate His love for us.

# MATTHEW 27

Now when morning had come, all the chief priests and the elders of the people took counsel against Jesus to put him to death: and they bound him, and led him away, and delivered him up to Pontius Pilate, the governor. Then Judas, who betrayed him, when he saw that Jesus was condemned, felt remorse, and brought back the thirty pieces of silver to the chief priests and elders, saying, "I have sinned in that I betrayed innocent blood."

But they said, "What is that to us? You see to it."

He threw down the pieces of silver in the sanctuary, and departed. He went away and hanged himself. The chief priests took the pieces of silver, and said, "It's not lawful to put them into the treasury, since it is the price of blood." They took counsel, and bought the potter's field with them, to bury strangers in. Therefore that field was called "The Field of Blood" to this day. Then that which was spoken through Jeremiah the prophet was fulfilled, saying,

"They took the thirty pieces of silver, the price of him upon whom a price had been set, whom some of the children of Israel priced, and they gave them for the potter's field, as the Lord commanded me."

Now Jesus stood before the governor: and the governor asked him, saying, "Are you the King of the Jews?" Jesus said to him, "*So you say.*"

When he was accused by the chief priests and elders, he answered nothing. Then Pilate said to him, "Don't you hear how many things they testify against you?"

He gave him no answer, not even one word, so that the governor marveled greatly.

Now at the feast the governor was accustomed to release to the multitude one prisoner, whom they desired. They had then a notable prisoner, called Barabbas. When therefore they were gathered together, Pilate said to them, "Whom do you want me to release to you? Barabbas, or Jesus, who is called Christ?" For he knew that because of envy they had delivered him up.

While he was sitting on the judgment seat, his wife sent to him, saying, "Have nothing to do with that righteous man, for I have suffered many things today in a dream because of him."

Now the chief priests and the elders persuaded the multitudes to ask for Barabbas, and destroy Jesus. But the governor answered them, "Which of the two do you want me to release to you?"

They said, "Barabbas!"

Pilate said to them, "What then shall I do to Jesus, who is called Christ?"

They all said to him, "Let him be crucified!"

But the governor said, "Why? What evil has he done?"

But they cried out exceedingly, saying, "Let him be crucified!"

So when Pilate saw that nothing was being gained, but rather that a disturbance was starting, he took water, and washed his hands before the multitude, saying, "I am innocent of the blood of this righteous person. You see to it."

All the people answered, "May his blood be on us, and on our children!"

Then he released to them Barabbas, but Jesus he flogged and delivered to be crucified. Then the governor's soldiers took Jesus into the Praetorium, and gathered the whole garrison together against him. They stripped him, and put a scarlet robe on him. They braided a crown of thorns and put it on his head, and a reed in his right hand; and they kneeled down before him, and mocked him, saying, "Hail, King of the Jews!" They spat on him, and took the reed and struck him on the head. When they had mocked him, they took the robe off him, and put his clothes on him, and led him away to crucify him.

As they came out, they found a man of Cyrene, Simon by name, and they compelled him to go with them, that he might carry his cross. When they came to a place called "Golgotha", that is to say, "The place of a skull," they gave him sour wine to drink mixed with gall. When he had tasted it, he would not drink. When they had crucified him, they divided his clothing among them, casting lots, and they sat and watched him there. They set up over his head the accusation against him written, "THIS IS JESUS, THE KING OF THE JEWS."

Then there were two robbers crucified with him, one on his right hand and one on the left. Those who passed by blasphemed him, wagging their heads, and saying,

"You who destroy the temple, and build it in three days, save yourself! If you are the Son of God, come down from the cross!"

Likewise the chief priests also mocking, with the scribes, the Pharisees, and the elders, said, "He saved others, but he can't save himself. If he is the King of Israel, let him come down from the cross now, and we will believe in him. He trusts in God. Let God deliver him now, if he wants him; for he said, 'I am the Son of God.'" The robbers also who were crucified with him cast on him the same reproach.

Now from the sixth hour there was darkness over all the land until the ninth hour. About the ninth hour Jesus cried with a loud voice, saying,

*"Eli, Eli, lima sabachthani?"* That is, *"My God, my God, why have you forsaken me?"*

Some of them who stood there, when they heard it, said, "This man is calling Elijah."

Immediately one of them ran, and took a sponge, and filled it with vinegar, and put it on a reed, and gave him a drink. The rest said, "Let him be. Let's see whether Elijah comes to save him."

Jesus cried again with a loud voice, and yielded up his spirit. Behold, the veil of the temple was torn in two from the top to the bottom. The earth quaked and the rocks were split. The tombs were opened, and many bodies of the saints who had fallen asleep were raised; and coming out of the tombs after his resurrection, they entered into the holy city and appeared to many.

Now the centurion, and those who were with him watching Jesus, when they saw the earthquake, and the things that were done, feared exceedingly, saying, "Truly this was the Son of God."

Many women were there watching from afar, who had followed Jesus from Galilee, serving him. Among them were Mary Magdalene, Mary the mother of James and Joses, and the mother of the sons of Zebedee. When evening had come, a rich man from Arimathaea, named Joseph, who himself was also Jesus' disciple came. This man went to Pilate, and asked for Jesus' body. Then Pilate commanded the body to be given up.

Joseph took the body, and wrapped it in a clean linen cloth, and laid it in his own new tomb, which he had cut out in the rock, and he rolled a great stone against the door of the tomb, and departed. Mary Magdalene was there, and the other Mary, sitting opposite the tomb.

Now on the next day, which was the day after the Preparation Day, the chief priests and the Pharisees were gathered together to Pilate, saying, "Sir, we remember what that deceiver said while he was still alive: 'After three days I will rise again.' Command therefore that the tomb be made secure until the third day, lest perhaps his disciples come at night and steal him away, and tell the people, 'He is risen from the dead;' and the last deception will be worse than the first."

Pilate said to them, "You have a guard. Go, make it as secure as you can." So they went with the guard and made the tomb secure, sealing the stone.

## PROPHECIES IN THIS CHAPTER

**Isaiah 52:13-53:12** – To Read this full text, see the bonus chapter after chapter 28.

**Psalm 22** – Psalm 22 is prophecy for Matthew 27. It is a prophetic scripture written about 600 years before Jesus lived and the entire Psalm is included as a bonus chapter, which appears after the Isaiah prophecy bonus chapter. You can go read Psalm 22 now, or wait to read it after the next two chapters.

**Isaiah 50:6** - I gave my back to those who beat me, and my cheeks to those who plucked off the hair. I didn't hide my face from shame and spitting.

**Psalm 38:11** – My lovers and my friends stand aloof from my plague. My kinsmen stand far away.

**Psalm 73:13** – Surely in vain I have cleansed my heart, and washed my hands in innocence,

**Jeremiah 18:16** – to make their land an astonishment, and a perpetual hissing; everyone who passes thereby shall be astonished, and shake his head.

**Daniel 9:12** – He has confirmed his words, which he spoke against us, and against our judges who judged us, by bringing on us a great evil; for under the whole sky, such has not been done as has been done to Jerusalem.

**Lamentations 1:12** – Is it nothing to you, all you who pass by?

Look, and see if there is any sorrow like my sorrow, which is brought on me,

With which The Lord has afflicted me in the day of his fierce anger.

**Lamentations 2:15** – All that pass by clap their hands at you.

They hiss and wag their head at the daughter of Jerusalem, saying,

Is this the city that men called The perfection of beauty, The joy of the whole earth?

**Psalm 27:12** – Don't deliver me over to the desire of my adversaries, for false witnesses have risen up against me, such as breathe out cruelty.

**Psalm 22:1** – My God, my God, why have you forsaken me? Why are you so far from helping me, and from the words of my groaning?

**Psalm 22:7-8** – All those who see me mock me. They insult me with their lips. They shake their heads, saying, 'He trusts in The Lord; let him deliver him. Let him rescue him, since he delights in him.'"

**Psalm 22:18** – They divide my garments among them. They cast lots for my clothing.

**Psalm 69:20-21** – "Reproach has broken my heart, and I am full of heaviness. I looked for some to take pity, but there was none; for comforters, but I found none. They also gave me gall for my food. In my thirst, they gave me vinegar to drink."

**Zechariah 12:10** – "I will pour on David's house, and on the inhabitants of Jerusalem, the spirit of grace and of supplication; and they will look to me whom they have pierced; and they shall mourn for him, as one mourns for his only son, and will grieve bitterly for him, as one grieves for his firstborn."

# WHY THESE PROPHECIES ARE IMPORTANT

The events that occurred in this chapter of Matthew, are detailed in the ancient prophecies. Psalm 22 and Isaiah 52:13–53:12 are long passages of text which describe these events.

Because we have not included verses from Psalm 22 in any of the prior chapters, I selected three particularly descriptive versus to include in this listing. I have not included the entire Psalm here, because it is included at the end of the book. As you read Psalm 22, it's easy to see the prophetic events described, which occurred in this chapter of the book of Matthew.

In addition to Psalm 22 and Isaiah 53, as deeply detailed descriptions of how the Messiah would be treated, we have a dozen additional prophecies cited here. Because these are all detailed prophecies, there isn't much need to explain each one individually. I'm confident you can see the correlation between these prophesies and the events which took place at Jesus' trial and crucifixion.

As you can see, these prophecies are important because they describe exactly what would happen to the Messiah. Because these prophecies all describe Jesus' treatment and the crucifixion in detail, we can rest assured all of these prophecies point toward Jesus as the true Messiah.

# WHAT STANDS OUT IN THESE PROPHECIES TO YOU?

# WHAT DO YOU THINK?

➢ What was it about Jesus that made the chief of priests and Elders hate Jesus and desire to put Him to death? Similarly, what makes some people really hate Christians today?

➢ A few days earlier, the multitude called Jesus the Son of David, and proclaimed, "Blessed is he who comes in the name of the Lord!" Then crowd turned on Jesus and began chanting, "Crucify Him!" What causes a multitude of people to turn into an angry mob and turn against someone they once respected? What kinds of sins and crimes occur whenever a multitude becomes an angry mob?

_____
_____
_____
_____
_____
_____
_____
_____

➢ Pilate washed his hands and proclaimed himself innocent of Jesus's death, yet he turned Jesus over to be crucified. What do you think God would say to Pilate about his innocence or guilt? What do you think Pilate's handwashing act accomplished?

_____
_____
_____
_____
_____
_____
_____
_____

➢ What sins and character flaws does a person demonstrate when they mock, belittle, and treat other people with contempt (like the religious leaders did to Jesus)? What groups of people mock and belittle others in society today? Are you part of any group(s) that belittles others?

_____
_____
_____
_____
_____
_____
_____
_____

- What made Jesus feel forsaken by God, even though Jesus knew God loved Him? Under what circumstances, if any, have you felt forsaken by God? What affect did those circumstances have on your faith?

_____
_____
_____
_____
_____
_____

- If Jesus told you He is the Son of God, then Jesus died, darkness fell, the Earth quaked, rocks split, tombs were opened, and Saints were raised from the grave, what feelings and questions would you have about Jesus being crucified?

_____
_____
_____
_____
_____
_____

# ACTION ITEM:

Did you notice, when Jesus died, others were resurrected? Chapter 27 says, "The tombs were opened, and many bodies of the saints who had fallen asleep were raised; and coming out of the tombs after his resurrection, they entered into the holy city and appeared to many." Reflect on these things:

How would you react if you saw relatives or friends appearing alive to you, even though you knew they died many years earlier? What do you think people were saying to each other when this happened?

If Jesus' death brought your relatives to life, would you have any doubt Jesus was the Messiah? If you would still have doubts, what would it take for you to truly believe, given the signs and prophecies God has already given us?

Whatever it would take to convince yourself, SEEK answers from God. Matthew 7:8 says, "For everyone who asks receives. He who seeks finds. To him who knocks it will be opened." Ask God to help you see His truth.

# WHAT'S NEXT?

In the next chapter, the Good News about Jesus begins to spread like a wildfire. The spreading of the news of Jesus has never stopped since His resurrection! Jesus gives His final instructions, and gives us a promise before He departs earth, as we await His second coming.

# MATTHEW 28

Now after the Sabbath, as it began to dawn on the first day of the week, Mary Magdalene and the other Mary came to see the tomb. Behold, there was a great earthquake, for an angel of the Lord descended from the sky, and came and rolled away the stone from the door, and sat on it. His appearance was like lightning, and his clothing white as snow. For fear of him, the guards shook, and became like dead men. The angel answered the women, "Don't be afraid, for I know that you seek Jesus, who has been crucified. He is not here, for he has risen, just like he said. Come, see the place where the Lord was lying. Go quickly and tell his disciples, 'He has risen from the dead, and behold, he goes before you into Galilee; there you will see him.' Behold, I have told you."

They departed quickly from the tomb with fear and great joy, and ran to bring his disciples word. As they went to tell his disciples, behold, Jesus met them, saying, *"Rejoice!"*

They came and took hold of his feet, and worshiped him.

Then Jesus said to them, *"Don't be afraid. Go tell my brothers that they should go into Galilee, and there they will see me."*

Now while they were going, behold, some of the guards came into the city, and told the chief priests all the things that had happened. When they were assembled with the elders, and had taken counsel, they gave a large amount of silver to the soldiers, saying, "Say that his disciples came by night, and stole him away while we slept. If this comes to the governor's ears, we will persuade him and make you free of worry."

So they took the money and did as they were told. This saying was spread abroad among the Jews, and continues until today.

But the eleven disciples went into Galilee, to the mountain where Jesus had sent them. When they saw him, they bowed down to him, but some doubted.

Jesus came to them and spoke to them, saying, *"All authority has been given to me in heaven and on earth. Go and make disciples of all nations, baptizing them in the name of the Father and of the Son and of the Holy Spirit, teaching them to observe all things that I commanded you. Behold, I am with you always, even to the end of the age."* Amen.

## PROPHECIES IN THIS CHAPTER

**Isaiah 62:11-12** – Behold, The Lord has proclaimed to the end of the earth, "Say to the daughter of Zion, 'Behold, your salvation comes. Behold, his reward is with him, and his recompense before him.'" They will call them The holy people, The Lord's redeemed. You will be called Sought out, A city not forsaken.

**Ezekiel 34:16** – I will seek that which was lost, and will bring back that which was driven away, and will bind up that which was broken, and will strengthen that which was sick: but the fat and the strong I will destroy; I will feed them in justice.

**Isaiah 40:9-11** – You who tell good news to Zion, go up on a high mountain. You who tell good news to Jerusalem, lift up your voice with strength. Lift it up. Don't be afraid. Say to the cities of Judah, "Behold, your God! Behold, the Lord God will come as a mighty one, and his arm will rule for him.

Behold, his reward is with him, and his recompense before him.

He will feed his flock like a shepherd. He will gather the lambs in his arm, and carry them in his bosom. He will gently lead those who have their young.

**Isaiah 56:4-7** – For The Lord says, "To the eunuchs who keep my Sabbaths, and choose the things that please me, and hold fast to my covenant: I will give them in my house and within my walls a memorial and a name better than of sons and of daughters. I will give them an everlasting name, that will not be cut off.

Also the foreigners who join themselves to The Lord, to serve him, and to love The Lord's name, to be his servants, everyone who keeps the Sabbath from profaning it, and holds fast my covenant;

I will bring these to my holy mountain, and make them joyful in my house of prayer. Their burnt offerings and their sacrifices will be accepted on my altar; for my house will be called a house of prayer for all peoples."

**Daniel 7:9-10** – I saw until thrones were placed, and one who was ancient of days sat: his clothing was white as snow, and the hair of his head like pure wool; his throne was fiery flames, and its wheels burning fire. A fiery stream issued and came out from before him: thousands of thousands ministered to him, and ten thousand times ten thousand stood before him: the judgment was set, and the books were opened.

**Daniel 7:13-14** – I saw in the night visions, and behold, there came with the clouds of the sky one like a son of man, and he came even to the ancient of days, and they brought him near before him. There was given him dominion, and glory, and a kingdom, that all the peoples, nations, and languages should serve him: his dominion is an everlasting dominion, which shall not pass away, and his kingdom that which shall not be destroyed.

**Daniel 10:6** – His body also was like the beryl, and his face as the appearance of lightning, and his eyes as flaming torches, and his arms and his feet like burnished brass, and the voice of his words like the voice of a multitude.

# WHY THESE PROPHECIES ARE IMPORTANT

The prophecies here in chapter 28 are not as clear as they were in previous chapters. I love these prophecies though, because they speak of the eternal nature of Jesus after He has been resurrected.

Isaiah 62 talks about the Messiah's people being called the Lord's redeemed and the people who follow Him will be called holy people. While everyone won't agree every Christian is a holy person, we are indeed called the Lord's redeemed. This passage also tells us the Messiah will be sought out. Jesus has been, and is continually being, sought by all kinds of people.

Ezekiel 34:16 is a reflective prophecy which describes how Jesus came to save the lost. He continues to bind up the brokenhearted, seek out people who are lost, and to call out to those who have been driven away by society. Jesus is a man of grace and justice, especially for the despondent and broken-hearted.

Isaiah 49 describes lifting up our voices with strength and not being afraid to say, "Behold, you are God!" Jesus' message was widely proclaimed immediately after his death and resurrection, because the resurrection was an unusual event *witnessed by more than 500 people*. As people today experience life changing growth and grace in their lives when they begin to follow Jesus, they continued to proclaim Jesus as the way of truth and life.

One of the key concepts which stands out in Isaiah 56:4-7 is the Sons and Daughters of the Messiah will have an everlasting name which will not be cut off. We join ourselves to the Lord, to serve Him, and to love Him forever. We follow the everlasting name of Jesus, we do it voluntarily, and we serve Him and love Him because of the grace, joy, and peace He brings into our lives.

The passages from Daniel 7 and 10 describe what the Messiah looks like on His throne in heaven. While we have not yet seen this with our very own eyes, we know from the Transfiguration event, Jesus was transformed into a glowing white figure. We also know Jesus said no one comes to the Father except through Him, and He will sit at the right hand of God the Father. He sits there as thousands upon thousands come before Him in judgment. Jesus has been given dominion over the Kingdom of all people, just as it was prophesied before He came. We will eventually see Him in all of His glory when we spiritually depart from this Earth.

# WHAT STANDS OUT IN THESE PROPHECIES TO YOU?

## WHAT DO YOU THINK?

- If you had been there when the bright white angel descended, rolled away the stone, then told you Jesus has risen and is going to Galilee, what affect do you think it would have on your faith?

- The women who first encountered Jesus after His resurrection were filled with fear and with great joy. Of what might you be afraid, if you were in those circumstances? What would make you joyful?

- Of what should the chief priests and the guards be afraid, since they were lying and scheming, rather than repenting for their lies and what they did to Jesus?

- The eleven disciples went to Galilee, just as Jesus requested, but the Bible says some of them doubted. What doubts do you think they had and why do you think they had doubts? What doubts might you have under the circumstances?

- Jesus's directive is to go and make disciples of all nations, baptizing them and teaching them. What are some ways you can continue making disciples in your community?

➤ What is your understanding of how Jesus fulfills His final declaration, *Behold, I am with you always, even to the end of the age*? Exactly how is Jesus with us always?

_____
_____
_____
_____
_____
_____
_____

## ACTION ITEM:

Think of someone you can disciple by helping them grow in their understanding of the Good News from Jesus. Discipling someone can be as simple as going through this study, one of my other studies, or any study with another person. As you study together and discuss your insights, questions, and seek to understand God's Word, you will help each other grow!

## WHAT'S NEXT?

Up next are two bonus chapters. Isaiah 53 and Psalm 22 are from the Old Testament, and they are filled with prophecy verses. In fact, these two books of the Bible are comprised almost entirely of prophecy. Therefore, they are a great way to finish out this Bible study.

Since you've been through Matthew's entire book about the life of Jesus on earth, it'll be easier for you to see the relationship between Jesus, His life, and these prophecies.

I hope you are as amazed by the detail in God's prophecies as I was when I first understood them. As you read, remember God gave these prophesies to us as THE SIGN of the Messiah hundreds of years before the Messiah was born. By God's Word, we can recognize exactly who is the Messiah.

Now that you know Jesus, take note of where the prophecies stand out as descriptions of Jesus and the events of His life.

Enjoy these amazing bonus chapters!

# BONUS: ISAIAH 52:13-53

BONUS CHAPTER:

Behold, my servant will deal wisely.

He will be exalted and lifted up, and will be very high.

Just as many were astonished at you (his appearance was marred more than any man, and his form more than the sons of men), so he will cleanse many nations.

Kings will shut their mouths at him: for they will see that which had not been told them; and they will understand that which they had not heard. Who has believed our message?

To whom has God's arm been revealed?

For he grew up before him as a tender plant, and as a root out of dry ground.

He has no good looks or majesty.

When we see him, there is no beauty that we should desire him.

He was despised and rejected by men, a man of suffering and acquainted with disease.

He was despised as one from whom men hide their face; and we didn't respect him.

Surely he has borne our sickness and carried our suffering; yet we considered him plagued, struck by God, and afflicted.

But he was pierced for our transgressions.

He was crushed for our iniquities.

The punishment that brought our peace was on him; and by his wounds we are healed.

All we like sheep have gone astray.

Everyone has turned to his own way; and God has laid on him the iniquity of us all.

He was oppressed, yet when he was afflicted he didn't open his mouth.

As a lamb that is led to the slaughter, and as a sheep that before its shearers is silent, so he didn't open his mouth.

He was taken away by oppression and judgment.

As for his generation, who considered that he was cut off out of the land of the living and stricken for the disobedience of my people?

They made his grave with the wicked, and with a rich man in his death, although he had done no violence, nor was any deceit in his mouth.

Yet it pleased God to bruise him.

He has caused him to suffer.

When you make his soul an offering for sin, he will see his offspring.

He will prolong his days and God's pleasure will prosper in his hand.

After the suffering of his soul, he will see the light and be satisfied.

My righteous servant will justify many by the knowledge of himself; and he will bear their iniquities.

Therefore I will give him a portion with the great.

He will divide the plunder with the strong; because he poured out his soul to death and was counted with the transgressors; yet he bore the sins of many and made intercession for the transgressors.

# PROPHECIES IN THIS CHAPTER

This entire bonus chapter, from the book of Isaiah, is a prophecy regarding the Messiah.

# WHY THIS BOOK OF PROPHECY IS IMPORTANT

These bonus scriptures show us God planned all that happened long before Jesus was born. From these Words of God's, we can look at people throughout the history of earth to look for the Messiah, as God described Him. We can see the Messiah is Jesus, if we believe history unfolded as it has been told.

# WHAT STANDS OUT IN THIS PROPHECY TO YOU?

_____
_____
_____
_____
_____
_____
_____
_____

# WHAT DO YOU THINK?

➤ In what ways has God's plan, power, and mystery been revealed to you through His prophecies?

_____
_____
_____
_____
_____
_____

➤ After reading the prophecies, do you fully believe the message of Matthew about Jesus? What do you feel certain about, and what do you struggle to believe?

_____
_____
_____
_____
_____
_____
_____

➢ Based on what you know, which passages in this bonus chapter clearly describe Jesus to you?

_____
_____
_____
_____
_____
_____

➢ As well as you are able, explain how Jesus' suffering for our sins gives us peace with God.

_____
_____
_____
_____
_____
_____
_____

➢ Why is it difficult to stop following your own way and begin following God's ways completely?

_____
_____
_____
_____
_____
_____

➢ Since we all violate God's commandments, we deserve the punishment Jesus received. Jesus paid for our sins by taking the punishment for us. Put into words the thoughts and feelings you have about Jesus giving you His gift of not having to suffer the punishment you deserve for your sins.

_____
_____
_____
_____
_____
_____

# BONUS: PSALM 22

BONUS CHAPTER:

My God, my God, why have you forsaken me?

Why are you so far from helping me, and from the words of my groaning?

My God, I cry in the daytime, but you don't answer; in the night season, and am not silent.

But you are holy, you who inhabit the praises of Israel.

Our fathers trusted in you.

They trusted, and you delivered them.

They cried to you, and were delivered.

They trusted in you, and were not disappointed.

But I am a worm, and no man; a reproach of men, and despised by the people.

All those who see me mock me.

They insult me with their lips. They shake their heads, saying,

"He trusts in The Lord. Let him deliver him.

Let him rescue him, since he delights in him."

But you brought me out of the womb.

You made me trust while at my mother's breasts.

I was thrown on you from my mother's womb.

You are my God since my mother bore me.

Don't be far from me, for trouble is near.

For there is no one to help.

Many bulls have surrounded me.

Strong bulls of Bashan have encircled me.

They open their mouths wide against me, lions tearing prey and roaring.

I am poured out like water.

All my bones are out of joint.

My heart is like wax.

It is melted within me. My strength is dried up like a potsherd.

My tongue sticks to the roof of my mouth.

You have brought me into the dust of death.

For dogs have surrounded me.

A company of evildoers have enclosed me.

They have pierced my hands and feet.

I can count all of my bones.

They look and stare at me.

They divide my garments among them.

They cast lots for my clothing.

But don't be far off, O Lord.

You are my help. Hurry to help me!

Deliver my soul from the sword, my precious life from the power of the dog.

Save me from the lion's mouth!

Yes, you have rescued me from the horns of the wild oxen.

I will declare your name to my brothers.

Among the assembly, I will praise you.

You who fear The Lord, praise him!

All you descendants of Jacob, glorify him!

Stand in awe of him, all you descendants of Israel!

For he has not despised nor abhorred the affliction of the afflicted,

Neither has he hidden his face from him; but when he cried to him, he heard.

My praise of you comes in the great assembly.

I will pay my vows before those who fear him.

The humble shall eat and be satisfied.

They shall praise The Lord who seek after him.

Let your hearts live forever.

All the ends of the earth shall remember and turn to The Lord.

All the relatives of the nations shall worship before you.

For the kingdom is The Lord's.

He is the ruler over the nations. All the rich ones of the earth shall eat and worship.

All those who go down to the dust shall bow before him, even he who can't keep his soul alive.

Posterity shall serve him.

Future generations shall be told about the Lord.

They shall come and shall declare his righteousness to a people that shall be born, for he has done it.

# PROPHECIES IN THIS CHAPTER

Most of Psalm 22 is prophecy about the Messiah.

# WHY THESE PROPHECIES ARE IMPORTANT

Like the previous bonus chapter, many of the verses in Psalm 22 are descriptive of the Messiah. Again, from these Words of God, we can look at historical figures throughout the history of our earth, and recognize the Messiah as God described Him. The prophecies in Isaiah 53 and Psalm 22 are two of the main reasons many people believe Jesus is the Messiah.

# WHAT STANDS OUT IN THESE PROPHECIES TO YOU?

# WHAT DO YOU THINK?

➢ Psalm 22 is a prophetic scripture written about 600 years before Jesus lived. Which passages in Psalm 22 do you recognize as descriptions of specific crucifixion events in Matthew 27?

_____
_____
_____
_____
_____
_____
_____
_____
_____

➢ Deuteronomy 18:22 tells us the words of God's true prophets come to pass. God gave us Isaiah 53, Psalm 22, and many prophecies within the Old Testament, to help us recognize the Messiah when He came to Earth. What affect do these prophecies have on your belief Jesus is truly the Messiah?

_____
_____
_____
_____
_____
_____
_____
_____

➢ Jesus suffered, was crucified, and died. We all suffer in life. We call out to God like Jesus did, but bad things still happen to virtually everyone at some point in their lifetime. What are some reasons you can think of as to why God lets bad things happen to those He loves, even His beloved Son?

_____
_____
_____
_____
_____
_____
_____
_____

➢ Since God created each of us, He has the right to do with us whatever He wishes (Ref: Romans 9:20-21). How does Jesus' life reflect both honor and dishonor? When you know you're created either for honor or dishonor, or for whatever purpose God has for your life, what feelings stir in you?

_____
_____
_____
_____
_____
_____
_____

➢ What has God provided or done for you, which amazes you? Write a short paragraph expressing your amazement and gratitude.

_____
_____
_____
_____
_____
_____
_____
_____
_____

➢ Describe God's righteousness as you would proclaim it to someone younger than yourself.

_____
_____
_____
_____
_____
_____
_____
_____

# WHAT'S NEXT?

Think about your faith in Jesus as the One and ONLY Messiah. If you believe He is, and you have accepted him as Lord over your life, you may want to get baptized, if you haven't been baptized already.

If you haven't accepted Jesus as Lord over your life, the next chapter will explain how you can ask Jesus to come into your life as your Lord and Savior. The next chapter is the final chapter of this study.

# WHAT'S NEXT?

Congratulations on completing the Gospel Book of Matthew. Now that you've met Jesus and studied prophecies about Him, you might wonder, "What's next?"

If you've prayed a prayer asking Jesus to be the Lord of your life, and asked him to help you overcome your sins, then your next step is getting baptized and seeking to know Him personally. Too many people rely on what others say, and they don't ever get to know Jesus for themselves.

Romans 16:18 warns us about people who lead others astray saying, "For those who are such don't serve our Lord, Jesus Christ, but their own belly; and by their smooth and flattering speech, they deceive the hearts of the innocent." If you don't get to know Jesus personally, then you will be open to being deceived.

Additionally, Jesus can't be nearly as effective in your life if you don't develop a relationship with Him. Everything that Jesus taught is important for your spiritual growth. Thus, it's critical for you to study everything taught in the Bible.

In Matthew 11:29-30, Jesus says, "Take my yoke upon you, and learn from me, for I am gentle and lowly in heart, and you will find rest for your souls. For my yoke is easy, and my burden is light." Studying Jesus helps build your faith in Him. Having faith in Him makes life less burdensome.

Do you remember the teachings Jesus gave about how your faith affects the outcome of your prayers? If you do, then you know it's important for you to have faith in Jesus in order to have effective prayers. The best way to strengthen your faith is to get to know Jesus deeply on a personal level.

You can get to know Jesus pretty well by reading all four of the Gospel books in the New Testament. They are the books titled Matthew, Mark, Luke, and John. Each one will give you different insights into who Jesus is and what He taught.

The four Gospels cover Jesus' actions and teachings in detail. Mark gives his account of Jesus' life through the eyes of Jesus' traveling companions—His disciples. Mark was the secretary who was the scribe for Apostle Peter's eye-witness account, and Mark knew several of the disciples.

Luke was a physician and a traveling companion of the Apostle Paul. Luke thoroughly investigated Jesus in order to give a detailed account of Jesus' life.

Matthew and John give their first-hand, eyewitness testimonies about Jesus. They were among the 12 chosen apostles of Jesus.

How will you get to know Jesus better? What are Jesus' expectations are for you and your expectations for your relationship with Jesus?

My recommendation is to dive into a study of the Gospel of Mark, with the Bible Study titled, *"Who Is Jesus?"* for your next study. It is the first book published in this Psalm 30 Publishing Journal Bible Study series, and it is the next Gospel book in the sequence of gospels in the Bible.

If you've already read the Gospel of Mark, you can find other journal Bible studies listed on my website at JournalBibleStudy.com.

Whether you study the New testament, the Old Testament, or read your Bible directly, you will find your knowledge and righteousness will continue to grow, as long as you keep studying your Bible! God's Word is living and it will bring you new insights and spiritual growth throughout your life.

When you study Jesus's teachings and God's expectations, prepare to be amazed. May God bless you throughout your journey. May the Lord give you great insights and inspiration, and develop you into a strong, spirited follower of Jesus Christ!

## DO YOU WANT TO JESUS TO BECOME YOUR LORD?

If you haven't already asked Jesus to come into your life as your Savior, it's really easy to do. All you have to do is ask Jesus to be your Lord and Savior. Here's what the Bible says about being saved:

- **Romans 10:9-10** says, "If you will confess with your mouth that Jesus is Lord, and believe in your heart that God raised him from the dead, you will be saved. For with the heart, one believes unto righteousness; and with the mouth confession is made unto salvation."

- **Romans 10:13** says, "Whoever will call on the name of the Lord will be saved." The name of the Lord is Jesus.

- **Mark 16:16** says, "He who believes and is baptized will be saved; but he who disbelieves will be condemned." Here, belief is the main key to being saved, but baptism is an act of faith for those who believe.

To be saved and have Jesus come into your life, it's as easy as believing Jesus is God's Son. With all sincerity, ask Jesus to save you and to become Lord in your life. You can do this easily by praying the following prayer:

*"Lord Jesus, I believe you are God's Son, and God resurrected you from the dead. Please come into my life as my Lord and Savior, and save me from my sins. In Jesus' name I pray, Amen."*

For a deeper understanding of the concept of being saved, the book of John, Chapter 3:14-21 (quoted below) should help you. Keep in mind, when these verses refer to 'light,' they mean Jesus, because He is the Light to the world:

"As Moses lifted up the serpent in the wilderness, even so must the Son of Man (Jesus) be lifted up, that whoever believes in Him should not perish, but have eternal life. *For God so loved the world, that He gave His one and only Son (Jesus), that whoever believes in Him should not perish, but have eternal life.* For God didn't send His Son into the world to judge the world, but that the world should be saved through Him (Jesus). The person who believes in Him (Jesus) is not judged. The person who doesn't believe has been judged already, because he has not believed in the name of the one and only Son of God. This is the judgment, that the light (Jesus) has come into the world, and men loved the darkness rather than the light; for their works were evil. For everyone who does evil hates the light, and doesn't come to the light (Jesus), lest his works would be exposed. But he who does the truth comes to the light (Jesus), that his works may be revealed, that they have been done in God."

May God bless you in the days ahead as you seek Jesus, His truth, and His light.

Going forward, I pray you will be greatly blessed whenever you spend time reading your Bible, praying, and fellowshipping with other believers. I pray you will find a church family you love, and you will seek to be baptized, if you haven't been already.

And remember always, if you prayed the prayer asking Jesus to be your Lord, because you believe in **Him, you are saved**!

## ♥ CONGRATULATIONS, and may God Bless YOU now and forever! ♥

*If you have a moment and would like to help fellow seekers, please leave an honest review describing this study on Amazon.com. Just search for "Is Jesus the Savior Journal Bible Study" on Amazon, select this book in the search results, and post your review in the reviews section. Your honest description will help other readers decide if this study is one that will help them grow.

# ABOUT THE AUTHOR

Sandra K. Cook (a.k.a. Sandy) became a Christian when a door-to-door evangelism came to tell her about Jesus. Sandy's life changed dramatically throughout the years that followed, although those changes didn't happen overnight.

Sandy was married at 19, widowed at the age of 22, lived in poverty, was assaulted, and a victim in a bank robbery, where she had a gun held to her head. In her early adulthood, Sandy was suicidal, struggled mightily with her self-esteem, and felt her life was pointless.

At the time of her first husband's death, Sandy began to read her Bible from cover-to-cover, deeply desiring to understand the purpose of life and to learn about God. Reading the Bible set Sandy's heart on walking with the Lord. She was gripped by the love God proclaims for each one of us, because she often felt unloved and unlovable.

In her life today, Sandy focuses on godly love, above all things, and seeks to help others feel and understand God's love, and to grow their fruit of the spirit. She believes everybody is more than just somebody... Everybody is God's Beloved Child, including YOU, my dear one!

The greatest joys in Sandy's life are spending time with her husband, sons, family, and her friends. Sandy loves reading to learn, studying the Bible, photography, and singing praise songs (although, you do not want to hear her tone deaf singing!)

Sandy earned her Degree of Divinity from the Christian Leaders Institute. She is a certified Biblical Life Coach, has a Master's Degree in Instructional Design, and is a life-long learner.

Sandy prays God will richly bless YOU in your life each and every day! ♥

# OTHER BOOKS BY SANDY K. COOK

WHO IS JESUS?

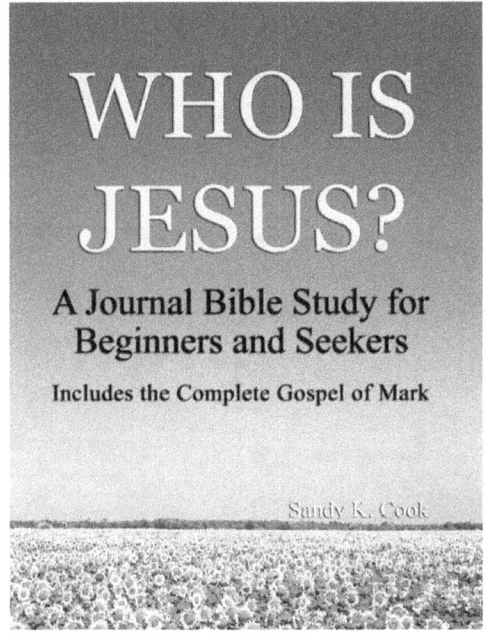

IS JESUS REAL?

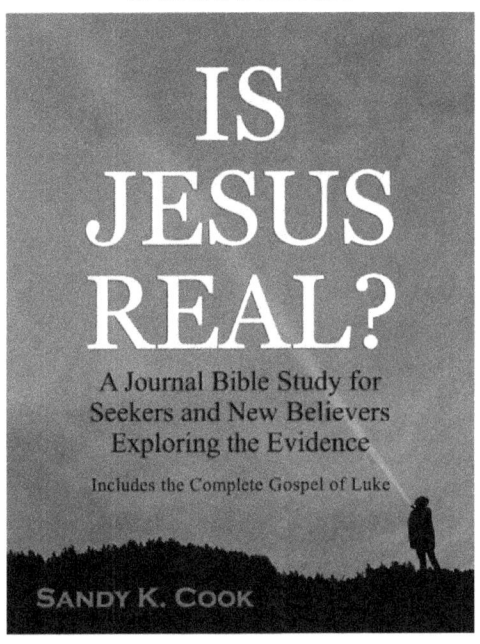

IS JESUS GOD?

BE A PERSON AFTER GOD'S OWN HEART

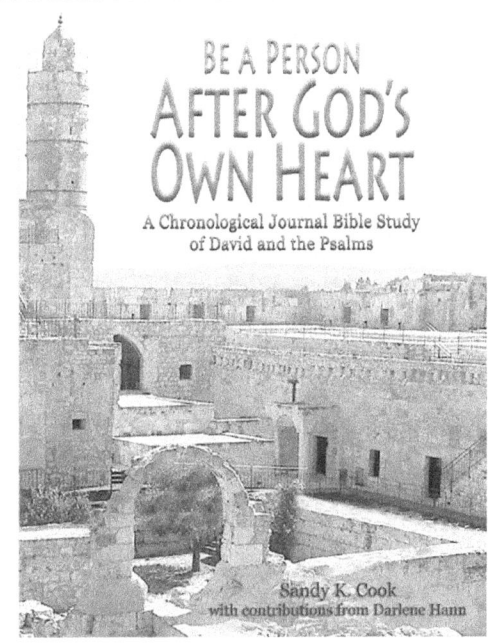

www.ingramcontent.com/pod-product-compliance
Lightning Source LLC
Chambersburg PA
CBHW081720100526
44591CB00016B/2439